# THE MYSTERIES
# OF HADITHA

# THE MYSTERIES
# OF HADITHA

*A Memoir*

M. C. ARMSTRONG

Potomac Books | *An imprint of the University of Nebraska Press*

Chapter 1 was previously published as "Axe" in the
*Wrath-Bearing Tree* (April 2018). Chapter 5 and a
portion of chapter 9 were previously published as
"Mysteries of Haditha" in *Consequence Magazine*
(Spring 2019). All photos by M. C. Armstrong.

Manufactured in the United States of America. ⊗

Library of Congress Cataloging-in-Publication Data
Names: Armstrong, M. C., author.
Title: The mysteries of Haditha: a memoir /
M. C. Armstrong.
Description: Lincoln NE: Potomac Books, an imprint
of the University of Nebraska Press, [2020]
Identifiers: LCCN 2020004158
ISBN 9781640123021 (hardback)
ISBN 9781640123915 (epub)
ISBN 9781640123922 (mobi)
ISBN 9781640123939 (pdf)
Subjects: LCSH: Armstrong, M. C. | Iraq War,
2003–2011—Personal narratives, American |
Iraq War, 2003–2011—Iraq—Ḥadīthah. | United
States—Armed Forces—Military life. | Embedded
war correspondents—United States—Biography. |
Embedded war correspondents—Iraq—Biography.
Classification: LCC DS79.766.A76 A3 2020 |
DDC 956.7044/342—dc23
LC record available at https://lccn.loc.gov/2020004158

Set in Huronia Latin Pro by Mikala Kolander.

But what about them?
—*My father*

# Contents

# Illustrations

# Acknowledgments

This book would not have been possible without the help of friends and strangers, as well as so many strangers who became friends. It certainly wouldn't have happened without the kindness and boldness of Tracy Crow. Tracy found me on an airplane heading home from Colorado and changed my life with a conversation. "Nothing is ever as it seems," Tracy always says, and she's right. Thank you, Tracy. And thank you to my father for showing me how to tell a story and for always challenging me and for being such a strong Papa Bear when our family needed you the most. I love you, Dad. Thank you to Diet for showing me Iraq and for serving our country with a brave heart and an open mind. Thank you to my brother, Andy, and my sister, Katee, for supporting the black sheep of the family. Thank you to Moni Basu for asking so many great questions. Thank you to Captain Al'a, Barry Barnes, Larry Becker, Maureen Bemko, Adrian Bonenberger, Robert Olen Butler, Carl Clymer, Susan Clymer, Paul Crenshaw, Hadis Daqiq, Julie Deery, Max Frazier, Warren Frazier, Dr. Joseph L. Graves, Corrie Gray, Betsy Greene, Jason Gulosh, Alan Hedrick, Mark Henkel, Joseph Hickman, James Tate Hill, Bill Hoffman, Corrie Hulse, Terry Kennedy, Phil Klay, George Kovach, Haley Mendlik, Nicholas Meriwether, Peter Molin, Christian Moraru, Michael Parker,

Chris Porter, Kevin Rippin, Emilie Rudy, Naima Said, Preston Schultz, Tommy Schultz, Grant Shuman, Karen Smith, Abigail Stryker, Tom Swanson, Karl VanOsten, and Andria Williams for your support and insights. Thank you to all of my inspiring students for continually pushing me to tell my stories and for asking so many questions. And, finally, thank you to the woman who made me a great deal a long time ago: "Tell me the truth and you won't get in trouble." I don't know if that's true, Mom, but it is TRUE. And so, I dedicate this book to you and all of the people who supported your crusades of truth and kindness. Thank you, Mom, for showing me truth matters, activism works, and that it's good to make friends with strangers.

# THE MYSTERIES
# OF HADITHA

# 1. MARCH 2008

## KUWAIT AND IRAQ

Why write? Draw naked chicks.
—GRAFFITI FROM THE WAR

I met a woman on my way to Iraq. Just before I stepped onto the midnight plane to Baghdad, she asked me what should have been a simple question:

"Who do you work for?"

Her name was Moni Basu. She was a journalist. She had thick dark hair plus an intense demeanor, and she wore a helmet labeled "Evil Media Chick." We were drinking coffee at a picnic table behind a beverage kiosk at the back of the Ali Al Salem base in Kuwait. Her traveling companion, a photographer named Curtis Compton, had caught shrapnel from an IED during a previous embed. A moment before, Moni had given me, a rookie journalist, an important Arabic term: *mutar saif.* It means lies, bullshit, or summer rain, a thing that just didn't happen in the desert.

I told her I worked for a magazine called CQ.

"GQ?"

"No. CQ."

"You write for *Congressional Quarterly?*"

The questions never stopped with Moni. She could smell the bullshit.

"*Convergence Quarterly*," I said. "It's a new magazine. This will be our first issue. We're sponsored by North Carolina A&T."

"You work at North Carolina A&T?"

1

I nodded nervously. I'm white. A&T is a historically black college in Greensboro, North Carolina. Many people argue that the student protest movement of the sixties began at A&T when four courageous young men conducted a sit-in at a Woolworth's lunch counter on February 1, 1960. This was the part of our history that we advertised to the world.

"Do you know who graduated from there?" Moni asked.

"Uh, Jesse Jackson?"

"Khalid Sheikh Mohammed?"

She said it like that, like a question, like she couldn't believe that I was here with her and didn't know this crucial fact. It was early March 2008, the fifth anniversary of the Iraq invasion. I'd been working at A&T as a lecturer in interdisciplinary writing for the past three years but didn't know a thing about Khalid Sheikh Mohammed.

"This is the guy who masterminded the attacks on 9/11," Moni said. "You don't know who Khalid Sheikh Mohammed is?"

Moni glanced at Curtis, who was applying a cloth to a lens with calm circular strokes. It was just beginning to dawn on me that I might be in way over my head, like maybe I was the man my father was afraid I was, a rube destined to die a ridiculous death in the coming days, my charred body hung from a bridge in some war-torn hamlet, men in loose-fitting garments cheering as my ashy corpse twisted in the wind. Or they'd put me in one of those orange jumpsuits and cut off my head, whoever "they" were.

I took a long sip of my coffee. Surely, whatever crush I had on Moni would not be reciprocated given my astounding ignorance about the war on terror. There I was, about to embed with Navy SEALs in Haditha, one of the most dangerous cities in Iraq, and I had no idea about the man who had started the very war I was trying to cover for a magazine that hadn't even released its first issue. I was twenty-four years old on 9/11. I did not question most of the official stories I heard emerging out of the early years of the war, and I certainly didn't think little Greensboro, North Carolina, had anything to do with this grand geopolitical narrative. Yes, I was the guy who had traveled seven thousand miles to learn that the mastermind of 9/11 had been educated in my own backyard.

"Excuse me," I said.

Rather than behave like a good journalist and question Moni relent-
lessly about KSM, I retreated to the bathroom to attend to suddenly
struggling bowels. I stared at the graffiti left by the troops:

*Chuck Norris's tears cure cancer. Too bad he never cries.*
*Here I sit, cheeks a'flexin, ready to unleash another Texan.*
*Here I sit, upon the crapper, ready to produce another rapper.*
*Can't wait to go home.*
*Have a nice war.*

They called my bus. I put on my army surplus helmet and bulletproof
vest, jotted down a few notes about the jokes in the toilet. I sat close to
Moni as the bus filled up. I didn't want to lose her. I felt like I needed
her, and I wasn't used to that feeling, that fear. I was the guy who loved
to live alone, the last of my friends to marry. But I didn't want to be left
alone in Iraq. On the drive to the plane I made small talk with Moni
about the record-breaking drought back home.

"It's so bad in Atlanta," she said, "that I keep a bucket in my shower
just so I can save enough water for my garden."

We walked across the tarmac and up the ramp into the loud, bloated
hull of a C-130 Hercules. It was Moni, Curtis, and I, plus four soldiers and
two contractors. The C-130 is an exposed experience, a cabin stripped of
padding and panel, the seats nothing more than net and pole, the lights
a dim red, white, and blue, the floor studded with traction pads. After the
plane took off, Moni fell asleep and so did one of the soldiers. Another
sat with his headphones blasting so loud, it sounded like spit was coming
out of his ears. I smelled grape Kool-Aid powder. I looked around at the
seemingly calm faces occasionally jostled by the turbulence. There was
no turning back. For the past six months I'd been obsessed with seeing
the war for myself and escaping the media-saturated mindfuck of Left
versus Right, peace versus war, WMDs, beheadings, and 9/11 conspiracy
theories. I wanted to see the thing for myself and escape the self-absorbed
American vortex of screens and social media, and now that I was here I
couldn't stop thinking about how blind I'd been to the very place I was
escaping: America—my own backyard.

Other than KSM, what else had I missed? Was I about to get kidnapped and beheaded, my father dropping to his knees in our front yard with photographers clipping pictures all around him, just like the dad of Nick Berg, the famous decapitated contractor? And were contractors—these men snoozing all around me—were they the bad guys like everybody said? Was America evil? And why were our troops so infatuated with Chuck Norris, a man who, at the time, I thought of as nothing more than an aging third-tier actor from a bunch of forgettable martial arts movies?

All the lights went out in the Hercules, the cabin a dark tunnel of jiggling multinational bodies as this massive airship began its spiral descent to Baghdad, the famous lights-out, corkscrew, roller-coaster free-fall approach being the military's way of evading RPGs and demonstrating to rookie journalists just how simultaneously colossal and agile America can be if it truly wants to keep itself a secret.

Baghdad seemed calm before dawn, more a dense constellation of sapphire lights than a bombed-out wasteland. I pressed my cheek against the glass of the Blackhawk. Here was one of the oldest cities in the world, Babylon itself on a Sunday morning. As a thirteen-year-old boy I'd seen Scuds and Patriot missiles on the news doing their duty, my country at war for the first time in this city down below, but Iraq meant nothing to me back then. In high school I owned a bong I named the Enola Gay. History was just a game, a trivial pursuit, a place to get names for marijuana paraphernalia. Now I was here, in the center of the mediated world, seated next to Moni and Curtis and two soldiers operating swivel guns as we flew over the dark crawl of the Tigris River.

We touched down on a slab of concrete behind a barricaded building known as LZ (Landing Zone) Washington. Apparently most of the soldiers at this chopper terminal for Green Zone activity were employees of a contractor firm known as Triple Canopy Security Solutions. Moni, Curtis, and I walked into the office with two soldiers who were in town for a court-martial.

The first thing I noticed inside LZ Washington was a photo on the wall, an autographed black-and-white shot of Chuck Norris next to the sign-in desk.

"What is the deal with all the Chuck Norris worship?" I asked Moni.

She shook her head and smiled, like I was paying attention to the wrong things. As we waited for our ride to CPIC, the Combined Press Information Center, I stepped closer to the Norris board, the little flapping scraps of pink and green Post-its framing the autographed photo, the Post-its scrawled with doggerel travelers had dedicated to this classic example of the Whitmanian American, that man who contains multitudes. Norris's life was actually quite remarkable, I started to realize at that moment. He was not only an actor but a former contractor, a highly decorated martial artist who formed an entire school of karate, and, on top of that, he was a devout Christian political wonk who'd recently taken over William F. Buckley's conservative column in hundreds of newspapers, railing against premarital sex, gay marriage, and other such signs of the apocalypse. The picture of Norris I saw posted in LZ Washington had him seated atop a motorcycle that might as well have been a white horse. Beneath were bits of wit such as

> Chuck Norris doesn't read. He stares at the book until it gives him information.
> Chuck Norris wears cowboy boots. They're made of real cowboys.
> Chuck Norris doesn't mow his grass. He dares it to grow.

I wrote down as many of these jokes as I could, determined to keep alive the lighter side of Iraq, but as we drove through the sunrise streets of Baghdad, I couldn't stop thinking about what Moni had said to me just before we'd gotten on the C-130.

*You don't know who Khalid Sheikh Mohammed is?*

How bad is America's amnesia, its will to blindness? And to what extent is that blindness connected to our sense of humor, our addiction to nervous, absurdist jokes? Was I the only one who didn't know the names of our enemies? How little did we know about "them"? From the back of a Humvee, I looked for faces. We passed by monolithic concrete barricades, the exhausted leers of street vendors pushing bales of blankets, a statue for the soldiers who'd fought against Iran in the grisly chemical weapons–fueled war of the 1980s. God, how did I not know that the man whose actions had prompted this whole "war on terror" was a graduate of the school where I taught? Was the gap a function of too many rips off the Enola Gay when I was a teenager? Was I the only American who was this clueless about the Global War on Terror?

Before I left for Iraq, I went through a massive battle with my father that nearly led to the deep-sixing of my trip. But once the old man realized his son was going to see the war no matter what, he took me on a walk and gave me some advice. He said that Operation Iraqi Freedom was just as much our civil war as it was theirs. He said all anybody talked about in the press was whether we were the good guys or the bad guys.

"But what about them?" he said. "Who's their good guy? Who's their George Washington? That's the story you want to find. Talk to *them.*"

That was my goal going in. I knew I had bigger fish to fry than the graffiti dedicated to Chuck Norris. But talking to actual Iraqis without intrusive oversight was easier said than done. After being in Iraq for more than a week, I still hadn't met a single Iraqi. On the eighth day of my tour, along with my military escort, who was a large mustachioed Mormon named Reynolds, I landed at Al Asad, a sprawling base that reminded me of summer camp, with soldiers jogging and playing volley-ball, fobbits (those who never leave the forward operating base, or FOB) zooming around in golf carts, a commissary store loaded with candy and chewing tobacco and cellophane-wrapped soft-core magazines display-ing pinup girls. Around three o'clock in the afternoon, under a shelter at the back of the base, as I was paging through a men's magazine, I heard a familiar voice.

"Eat Boy!"

I looked up from my picnic table and ran down to the barricaded cul-de-sac where my SEAL platoon had parked their Humvees. I hugged my old friend, now the lieutenant for this platoon that was actually a Joint Special Operations Force (mostly SEALs mixed with contractors, CIA, and U.S. Army Rangers). Diet was a guy I'd known since I was five years old. He looked different, his thick, bristly mustache designed to create an air of gravitas and power—what the Iraqis called *wasta—*

but to me it was pure comedy, a nod to the porn stars of the seventies or perhaps the viceroys of nineteenth-century colonial England, or to Panama Jack.

"Nice 'stache," I said.

Diet commented on the disproportion between the hair on my face and the hair on my head. Whereas he was growing a mustache, I was growing a beard, having learned from him that while mustaches suggest power to Iraqis, the beard suggests a holy man.

"You're in the back," Diet said, as we stepped toward a Humvee with the name Leonidas spray-painted on the back. Leonidas was an ancient Spartan king, as well as a fictional character from a recent movie, *300*, which followed one Spartan unit's heroic exploits during the Battle of Thermopylae. According to historical legend and the movie, the Spartans died valiantly fighting against King Xerxes and his Persian horde, the Spartan story told only because Leonidas was wise enough to send a man named Dilios away from the platoon on the night before the decisive battle, so that he—Dilios—might tell the story of the soldiers' bravery to the masses.

"We're driving?" I said.

Diet nodded and smiled. I was surprised and pleased, and scared shitless. I'd enjoyed the aerial views of Iraq and the absence of Iraqis but was growing a bit suspicious of the embedding strategy, the careful hopscotch from base to base, the way we avoided all the spaces between, the people.

"You scared?" Diet asked.

"Should I be?" I said.

"No," he said. "That's part of the story here."

I put on my helmet and ceramic-plated vest. Complacency Kills, said a spray-painted sign on the edge of Al Asad. A soldier named B. Dubbs was driving as we passed beyond the wire—the concertina and concrete barriers. Diet passed back a tin of Copenhagen. I threw in a pinch, feeling like high school, about to go rallying through the woods of rural Virginia on a winter day, except we weren't entering a state forest or the rutted lanes of an apple orchard. This was a war zone.

Diet had described Haditha to me as the West Virginia of Iraq, a triad of tribal villages 150 miles northwest of Baghdad. Unemployment was 70 percent. There was desert everywhere, many of the people making a living the way they had for thousands of years: fishing and farming, ghostly figures herding goats on the smoke-plumed horizon. There were men in robes selling what looked like lemonade from cheap, collapsible roadside tables.

"That's gas," Diet said.

I nodded my head. Children ran along the shoulder with their hands outstretched. We threw them candy, Jolly Ranchers. I felt good. I loved the way the desert sky was skinning my eyes, the taste of my fresh chaw and its fiberglass shards tearing through my gums, the feeling of sharing a buzz with Diet in this surreal landscape that seemed to go back and forth between war-torn and exotic, novel and vivid on the one hand, tragic and impoverished on the other. I listened to the gobble of radio communications, smelled the sweat of the men, saw fruit stands pass by along the road, date palms and eucalyptus, a graveyard of jets, a black, burned-out hulk of a sedan on the shoulder a reminder that I was not in the Disney version of Iraq anymore and that at any moment one of these swaddled and stoic-faced roadside strangers might decide to press a button on a cell phone he'd converted into a remote control and thereby remind me that not everybody shared the children's enthusiasm for the foreigners with their tanks and their sunglasses and their gargantuan guns and their swollen lower lips.

I tried to keep my head in the moment as we approached Haditha, my vision of the world at that moment an opaque, dust-smeared profile of Diet riding shotgun, his face a single sunglass eye and the edge of that thick mustache, a wire coming out of his ear, his lips mutely mouthing orders into a mic as we passed through a gate, and then we could suddenly see a lake to our left and the Euphrates valley to our right down below, this ancient river of grade-school lore now a roaring spout from the concrete jaws of a massive dam, the slabby Soviet architecture and the sulfurous smell of the Haditha dam not enough to mute the feeling of ancient resonance, the awe of seeing distant cities of mud huts clustered behind palms on the east and west banks, a vast desert stretching out forever on the southern horizon, no billboards anywhere.

"Can we go for a swim?" I asked.

"You do not want to swim in there," Diet said.

I wondered what that meant. Was the river polluted or was he wisely discouraging the appearance of recreation, a spring break scene of buddies, of privileged white men splashing around in sacred waters while unemployed dark people downstream were cutting each other's heads off? I've always been a sucker for symbolic baths, halfhearted ablutions. When I see a new body of water, I want to swim. I kept telling myself to shut the fuck up, to remember the wisdom of Mark Twain: "It is better to keep silent and be thought a fool than to speak and remove all doubt."

We parked the Humvees, stepped out, and were greeted by a pack of sand-colored mongrel dogs that threaded their way through our dispersing ranks. I gave one a tentative pat, stretched my legs, and spit out my dip, then looked around the base at black, missile-shaped tubes of inflatable boats leaning up against the concrete barriers that fortified the borders, red and green storage containers forming a wall against the southern end of the camp, an empty plywood watchtower like the first leg of a Trojan horse.

"Who's on the other side?" I asked Diet, as we stood on the bank of the river and looked across at the camp on the other side. He said this was where the contractors slept. Sure enough, I saw the letters KBR sprayed in red on a concrete wall, a few extremely thick men milling around. KBR (Kellogg Brown & Root) was a subsidiary of Vice President Dick Cheney's old company, Halliburton.

"What do they do?" I said.

"They more or less take care of the trash," Diet said.

The great secret of my time in Iraq, I sometimes think now, was the smoke I inhaled from that trash, the burn pits KBR ran and the rash of scary symptoms discovered in soldiers and Iraqis. But I'm getting ahead of myself.

Diet showed me the trailer where I could take a shower, and he then ushered me into a maze of corrugated storage containers. I followed him across a wooden plank past a dark, empty plywood room. Behind this was another row of these metal containers, the "Conex" boxes that served as the sleeping quarters for his men, each door sprayed with their nicknames, monikers like Lurch and Tree. Diet's door was marked by two big black letters: LT.

"Damn. Not bad," I said, as I walked inside and beheld strands of Christmas lights forming vines above a red bed and a wall decorated with an ornate tribal tapestry, the pattern a pointillist spread of teal and brown leaves. Trunks of care-package goodies lay everywhere, a MacBook on a desk under a reading lamp. Behind Diet's computer sat a black-and-white photo of his father from his time in the U.S. Marine Corps during Vietnam. Above the photo were Diet's books, including a tattered copy of William Faulkner's *Flags in the Dust*.

As Diet took off his gear, I sat down in his black swivel desk chair and read through his Faulkner. I came across a line on a page that had been dog-eared, a passage I wrote down for some reason: "When a feller has to start killin' folks, he most always has to keep killin' 'em. And when he does, he's already dead hisself."

"You hungry?"

"What do you think?" I said.

"I know. Stupid question."

He laughed. Eat Boy is always hungry. Diet offered me one of his care-package nutrition bars, something with flax and honey and other progressive ingredients. It felt good to eat, to take off my shoes, to savor for a second the sense—the illusion—of finally having arrived.

"Fucking Eat Boy," he said.

"Bet you never thought this was going to happen," I said.

"No," he said. "To be honest. I didn't."

I looked at the cutouts of women from *Maxim* magazine he'd taped to the walls. He had a white dry-erase board on the back of his door.

"Let's come up with a list of five stories," he said.

He wanted me to focus on the SEAL mystique, the Iraqi SWAT team they'd trained, and the reduction in violence that many were calling the Al Anbar Awakening. When I said I could find my stories on my own, he looked skeptical, or perhaps paternal is the better word, or maybe the expression was close to the same look Moni produced when I asked about Chuck Norris and told her I'd never heard of KSM. All three of them—Diet, my dad, and Moni—knew I knew nothing, and I suspect they all thought this was to my detriment. Looking back now, I wonder if there hadn't been a certain advantage to my naivete.

"Just out of curiosity," I said, "why do there have to be five?"

"It's a good number, Eat Boy. One story a day for a full workweek."

Three months earlier, after our local newspaper had backed out on sponsoring me because my father had threatened their editor (his patient) with a lawsuit if anything happened to me while I was in Iraq, Diet had called me from Haditha and challenged me to "be a man," to make the trip happen in spite of my father's resistance. After all, I wouldn't be the only American to fake his way into this war if I, say, came up with a magazine of my own. So I was proud of this, my American ingenuity. But as Diet stood there telling me what stories to write, I felt like he was meddling and inviting me to cross a line I would not be proud to cross. I liked the idea of five stories, but I wanted to find the five.

"I wanna meet some Iraqis," I said.

"Right now?"

"Yeah."

"You wanna meet Captain Allah?"

"Yes, I wanna meet Allah."

That's how the name first sounded to me—Captain Allah—Captain God. Like, sure, let's go straight to the top. I had no idea who Captain Allah was, but he sounded important. Diet and I walked back through the maze of trailers that finally spilled out into the open air of the Iraqi night, where I witnessed some of the brightest stars I'd ever seen, the lighting of the base kept deliberately low, the vast miles of desert all around us offering no diffusing glow to the constellations, Orion stippled with a dress of chain-mail armor, stars below his belt I'd never seen before. I stopped to spin around in the cool night air as if I were stoned, wanting to absorb every detail: the tall black SEAL walking out of the shower hut with a towel around his neck, the mongrel dogs play-fighting down at the southern end of the base by the red punching bag hanging beneath the watchtower.

We walked into the room of one of the platoon's translators, a thick-bearded Jordanian named Rami who had a large American flag posted over his bed in the same fashion that Diet had a tribal tapestry tacked over his. Cutout pictures of women in skin-tight apparel modeling machine guns dotted Rami's walls.

Diet was briefing Rami on what was about to happen and I was admiring a photo of a blonde woman in a black dress wielding a black rifle when a tall man with a feathered mullet and a gold tie walked through the door, his entrance worthy of a sitcom scene. I half expected a studio audience to explode into a roar of applause. He was gangly, a silver pen clipped to his left breast pocket, his white dress shirt and olive suit freshly ironed, his eyes moving left to right in a furtive display of awareness and anxiety that evoked Kramer's character from *Seinfeld*. But this was unhinged, unrehearsed. Here was a man like me, who did not know his role, and no feature of his appearance suggested this more than the feathered mullet.

"Matt, this is Capt. Al'a Khalaf Hrat. He's the leader of the Iraqi SWAT team we've been training over the past few months."

"Assalamu alaikum," I said, rather proud of myself for remembering this rote greeting.

I shook the man's hand, felt a strong calloused grip. He responded with a deep voice and an abridgement of the conventional crib sheet Arabic greeting: "Salaam."

He took off his jacket, revealing a shoulder holster, two pistols tucked beneath his arms. He took that off as well, spoke at length, looking back and forth from me to Diet, never once looking at Rami, which I thought was "interesting," as they say.

"He wants to know where you're from," Rami said.

Either Arabic is the most inefficient language in the world or Captain Al'a wanted to know more than just where I was from. Rami wore a tan jumpsuit with an American flag above his left breast. I was anxious, aware that a lot was going to be lost in translation. I had my journal in my hands with all of the questions I wanted to ask but felt tempted, as I almost always do, to improvise, to throw my notes aside and go with the feeling of the moment.

For the first time in my life I was not only in Iraq, but I was finally sitting with an Iraqi, the leader of a SEAL-trained SWAT team. Who was this guy? Was he merely a dark version of the SWAT cops on TV, these romantic figures who always get to break the law in the name of the law? Was I dealing with the alpha dog, the badass, a rogue cop, the sort of man who made his own rules? I kept getting this comic vibe from Captain Al'a, the ghost of the American mullet and its connotations of "I don't give a fuck, throw me another beer" mentality.

After telling Al'a that I was from a town close to Washington DC, I decided to forget my questions about statistics and George W. Bush and the fifth anniversary of the invasion and the Al Anbar Awakening and ask about his hair. I said I liked his mullet. Added that I understood different hairstyles meant different things to different people, that the mustache was supposed to mean power and the beard holiness. "But what does the mullet mean?"

I exchanged a quick look with Diet, who shook his head in crestfallen disbelief. Captain Al'a crinkled his eyes and also looked toward his boss, perhaps not expecting the interrogation with the American journalist to broach such serious subjects as the symbolic significance of a mullet. I felt like such an amateur. I wondered what Moni would have asked. More than a hundred thousand Iraqis had already been killed in the war and I was asking questions about hair care. I looked down at Al'a's feet, determined to get serious with the next question, scolding myself for my improvisational approach, my belief in naivete perhaps nothing more than the sophist's justification for laziness, a tragicomic foreshadowing of the America to come. In the seconds between my question and Al'a's answer, I noticed the captain wore ankle-high socks. His trousers held a sharp, pleated crease and pinstripes. He removed a pack of cigarettes from his breast pocket and offered me one.

I took it. We both lit up. And then he began to talk, his deep voice drawn into higher registers by the frenzy of his thoughts, glottals and hisses clashing, Rami listening from his desk, the captain seated on the translator's bed, Diet standing over us. When Al'a finished speaking, he took a deep inhalation and blew a clean, two-pronged stream of smoke out of his considerable nostrils, his face—with wide eyes and large nose—a bit reminiscent of the Muppet character Gonzo.

"He says that his men are not afraid of death," Rami said. "He says that in some cities his haircut is not allowed, that it means a man is gay, and if you are gay you can get killed. But he is not gay. He just does what he wants. He is not afraid of death. He has lost eight family members, three brothers kidnapped and killed. His uncle, who was the police chief—he and his three children were murdered. It has been a terrible time for Hadithans. Hundreds of people leaving the city for Syria and elsewhere. Refugees. There was a man, an insurgent, who spoke to an American in public so everyone could see. Fifteen minutes this man and the American talk so everyone can see. Then the insurgent goes and kills an old innocent man, a barber. What do you think people thought? Do you understand the game they play? You cannot be afraid of death."

Lately I've given a lot of thought to this moment, the story that emerged out of that question about hair. Many of the men we armed in Al Anbar, men like Al'a, joined the Islamic State. Many of those who did not continued to flood Syria, contributing to the destabilization of that country and its civil war, which continues to this day. So I've thought about Al'a's words a lot, his story, the flood of death in his family. I've thought about these words specifically: "You cannot be afraid of death." This value, what some used to call bravery, has not aged well in the twenty-first century, or at least the American version. Sometimes we now call people who embrace death "cowards." The absence of fear in the face of death runs totally counter to the American way of life and the way it's so structured around careerism and self-interest, retirement and insurance and health care, keeping people alive into their nineties, banking their bodies in the faceless retirement communities we find near our beaches and deserts, Florida and Arizona.

That night I looked into the spaniel calm of the captain's eyes as another stream of smoke issued from his nose. A million thoughts were rushing through my head. I thought of Native Americans, the ones who got the haircuts and joined us, the ones who didn't, the Shawnee who occasionally came to dance at my elementary school when I was a child. Was I engaged in a timeless rite in that moment, sharing tobacco with a brave?

How ironic was it that the white man, or at least the white man's corporation, was now the one to provide the tobacco? And who truly was the "savage" in this game of drones and beheadings, snipers, IEDs, and WMDs? What would you think if you were in the captain's shoes, an Iraqi man working with Americans in the heart of a war that might well be illegal and might possibly (and simultaneously) produce positive but unintended consequences, your every move fraught with the implications of poverty versus complicity? A simple conversation could cost you your life.

I felt a tremendous surge of affection and pity for Captain Al'a. We continued the interview. I learned that he belonged to the tribe known as the Jughayfi. He was the son of a worker at a local oil refinery. He had witnessed the Iran-Iraq War and thereafter the first war with the United States. For a long time, like most Iraqis, his hatreds were pure, thoroughly controlled by an oppressive regime and its lockstep media, a government that kept tight control over the textbooks in the schools.

"You were not allowed to think," Al'a told me. "Everything was military."

God, I wanted to drink a beer with this guy and tell him about what it had been like the last five years in America, with generals galore on TV, generals on the radio, CIA on NBC, assassins on Fox, anchorwomen cheerleading the war, military budgets exploding, everybody in the country shaving their head like yours truly, everybody with their Support Our Troops bumper stickers and tree ribbons, every chickenhawk politician suddenly with polished flag pins posted on their lapels, country musicians turned into jingoistic sycophants for the war machine, everybody every day constantly reminded by the streaming ticker on the TV that we were living in Code Orange and it was all the fault of people like Captain Al'a.

"How have things changed?" I asked him.

"Come downtown with me," he said. "Come see the souk. It used to be so small you could fit it into the back of a truck. Now it's like, it's like— it's like Europe. It's like Paris."

Rami laughed, said to me, "Matt, it's not that nice. Definitely not Paris."

"You should come to the market," Al'a said.

I looked to Diet like a teenage son begging permission from his father to go to a party with the older guys, an archetypal convertible revving in the driveway. Diet looked back at me like I wasn't quite ready to take that ride—a long, pointed blink.

"Don't worry, Eat Boy," he said. "We're going downtown tomorrow."

I was terrified—thrilled, intoxicated by war, confident in the seal of my spectatorial membrane, my security detail. I'd never been "downtown" in a place where barbers were murdered in the streets, a city where there were "attacks" every day. I felt like I was doing the right thing. I was finally getting around to my father's advice. I was talking to an Iraqi. But there was still a veil over the scene, a translator and a lieutenant, concrete barriers everywhere outside. To go "downtown"—that might actually qualify as reality, an authentic "beyond the wire" glimpse of Iraq. Hot dog! Come on, Daddy-o! Can't I see beyond the walls?

Diet told me to wrap it up. I suggested a photograph with the captain before calling it a night. Then, in a moment I'll never forget, Captain Al'a stood up and brandished a small bottle of Axe cologne. This baffled me. We'd been sitting incredibly close the whole evening and not once had he broken out the cologne. Smell, of course, is not conveyed in a photograph, so why the hell would a man spray himself with cologne prior to a photo? To comb one's mullet or tighten one's tie—this I understood. But as I flew back to the United States a week later, I couldn't stop thinking about this final gesture. Why had this man with a mullet sprayed himself so profusely with cologne before locking arms with me? Was this a custom my crib sheets had neglected to apprise me of? And why, of all colognes, was he wearing Axe? More important, why do I focus on trivial things like haircuts and colognes when there are body counts and ideologies and elections and secret prisons everywhere?

Perhaps the answer is simple. I don't know. I'm a coward. I'm an American idiot. But maybe that's too easy, modesty to the point of dishonesty and disavowal. So let me try to step it back. One thing most Americans know is this: Axe is the Walmart of colognes. Axe is the most aggressively advertised cologne/body spray in the American marketplace, a cheap and strong smell for young men who take their cues from the media. Axe is what we advertise to the young after advertising Viagra and Cialis to the old and Coke to all. Axe is the smell of America if you're sniffing for the scent while watching our most popular programs in Iraq. Just as I was looking in the dark for Iraq, perhaps Iraq was looking for me too. Maybe Iraq, too, was befuddled by the multitudes Chuck Norris contained, the strange mixed messages of our muse and our media. Maybe Iraq and Captain Al'a were as confused about us as we were about ourselves. Whatever the case may be, I think it's safe to say that I'll never forget Captain Al'a, the way his mullet brushed my bare scalp as we wrapped arms for the photo, his locks dusting me with a musk laced with body odor and American tobacco, his ribs for a moment in contact with mine, their texture uncovered by his absent holster, the awareness of those bones sharpened by that strong American smell.

# 2. SEPTEMBER 2007

## AMERICA

Chuck Norris doesn't consider it
sex unless the woman dies.

—GRAFFITI FROM THE WAR

My journey to Iraq began with the end of my engagement to a woman named Karen. Karen had been conceived in rape, raised in a cult (the Worldwide Church of God), and was homeless by the age of fifteen. When I first met her in 2004, I had no idea how powerful trauma could be or how she was about to scramble the story of my life. The tale of my time in Iraq is both a love story and a ghost story, a thing that goes back and forth, perhaps a fairly typical account of how a woman both haunts and inspires a man's journey into war. During the day on Christmas Eve 2006, after a heated fight with her in front of my family, I called off our engagement. But ten months later, while driving home from work, I decided to do a drive-by of the old house Karen and I used to share in Greensboro. It was a little beige one-story ranch with a broken solar panel on the roof.

If Karen wasn't home, I was going to pull into the driveway, step inside the fenced-in backyard, and pay a visit to Evildoer, Karen's little Jack Russell, whom I'd I come to think of as my own. In that eight-hundred-square-foot house we'd kept two dogs (Evildoer and Kira), two cats (Jonah and Judas), a turtle (Tallulah), and a boa constrictor (Hank). But Evildoer was by far my favorite, and I felt like I needed to see him before heading back to Colfax, where I was now living with an old friend in a small house on the edge of a holler so remote that at midnight, every night, you could hear the bray of a donkey from our neighbor's farm.

I made the turn onto Joan Avenue, noticed a vehicle I didn't recognize in the old driveway, a gray Cherokee. I felt envy and pain flood my veins, imagined things I didn't want to imagine, that typical cinematic scene of the man discovering his girlfriend naked with a stranger in the middle of the afternoon, except I wasn't the boyfriend anymore. I had no right to be there. There would be no visiting Evildoer that day, no serendipitous encounter with my ex. So I turned around, got back on Battleground Avenue, and twenty minutes later I pulled onto the gravel drive that led past the horse farm and back to "the cabin," the home I shared with my colleague at North Carolina A&T, Joe.

Joe was gone. He always went to an AA meeting after work. I dropped my backpack, stepped into the kitchen, and noticed a puddle of piss on the brown brick–patterned linoleum. I checked the answering machine. There was a call from my mother and another from Diet, my old childhood friend, a man whose nickname in high school had been an obvious contrast to my own: Eat Boy. Diet was discipline. I was gluttony. Diet was the Navy SEAL. I was the guy still trying to get a rock 'n' roll band together and living week to week. I was the guy who had signed on to a loan so Karen could buy a Prius, a purchase that, among other things, was already coming back to haunt me. Many evenings I would return home to find letters from the bank, reminders of debts we couldn't pay, the fact that both our names were on the account a constant reminder of what could have been.

"Eat Boy," Diet said on the message. "I'm leaving in a week. Call me."

Here was another life, an old friend on the verge of taking a journey. I thought about Diet, how the last time we'd seen each other was climbing this ten-thousand-foot mountain called Dick's Peak and how from the rocks at the top we'd seen a neighboring peak spitting smoke, the distant white puff an hour later a 9/11-sized billow fingering its way down into the valley in what was the beginning of one of the largest forest fires in the history of California. I remembered how peaceful I'd felt as we'd marched out of the woods, the smoke at our back, the calm and clarity of danger a thing for which I'd always been a bit of a sucker.

I didn't yet have a cell phone. I say this only to paint a clear picture of that moment in "the cabin." I was standing in a brown linoleum kitchen staring at bills and a cordless phone and a puddle of urine from my room-mate's dogs. I muttered and cursed. I mopped up the piss. I frittered around the house, made myself some pasta. I wanted to call my mother back first, but I felt beat and I didn't like talking to my mother when I felt that way. She'd been diagnosed with ovarian cancer two years earlier. My grandfa-ther had just been diagnosed with leukemia. My relationship with Karen was over. Sometimes it was like I could feel the bell jar descending, the walls coming down, the incapacitating depression just one more shock away. One of the reasons I'd nearly gone through with my engagement to Karen was the desire for one final family reunion, a wedding in which my mother and grandfather might be able to see me married off, as if by saying "I do," I might be able to allay some worry within the clan, tie up a collective narrative strand, let everybody know that now it was time to start worrying about the next generation.

Well, that wasn't the way it played out. I deferred. This increasingly seemed to be my approach to life: wait, delay, hold out. Question the whole enterprise. I picked up my guitar and played a few tunes, checked in with the world on my laptop. Maybe I watched some porn or an old Grateful Dead video or some footage from the war. The sun went down. I heard the snap, crackle, and pop of the gravel—Joe returning from his meeting.

I still hadn't called my mother. Or Diet. And I felt like it was all Joe's fault, the fact that I didn't feel like talking to anybody due to the anger that was a function of those puddles of piss in the kitchen. Joe had res-cued me, allowed me to live in that house out in the woods after all my plans for a wife and kids had fallen through, but still, in spite of this, I would sometimes blame him for my pain and would truly have to sum-mon patience and goodwill just to keep from accosting him for something as petty as a puddle of piss.

"Hey," Joe said.

He tossed his bags on the busted-up brown vinyl loveseat that sat per-pendicular to the front door of the house. He looked a little exhausted himself. I don't think either of us had recognized the challenges we'd face teaching English in an experimental interdisciplinary department at a historically black college under the leadership of a black boss whose central academic argument was that race, biologically, doesn't exist. We were constantly being told by our colleagues that our days were numbered.

"I saved you some pasta," I said.

I felt like a parody of a frustrated wife as I ushered Joe into the kitchen to show him the clotted mound of spaghetti that looked more like a lacquered tract of intestines than a meal fit for a man.

"Thanks," he said.

Although it's tempting to remember that word of thanks as insincere for the sake of comedy, the fact is, it seemed sincere, which is to say, Joe *always* seemed sincere. He was a great friend. I didn't bring up the piss or work. We talked for a while at the kitchen table about how shitty we both felt. I told him I'd done a drive-by. He shook his head.

"Been there," he said.

Which was all I needed to hear. I was not alone. Joe had gone through a divorce right around the time I'd met Karen. He knew what it was like to be haunted by regret and jealousy, the specter of the responsible men we were supposed to be. When he got a call on his cell phone from a guy in the program, I decided maybe it was time for me to appear as if I too had a life, that is, people to talk to, which technically I did. But instead of calling my mother and confronting all the emotions—the fears—that came with those calls, I called Diet. It was after ten, around dinnertime out in San Diego, where he lived in a condo a few blocks from the beach.

"Eat Boy," he said.

I took the cordless outside, paced around in the gravel driveway as we caught up with each other, the stars in Colfax brighter than they were in Greensboro, the canopy of trees overhead almost as dense as a rainforest. I heard the far-off sound of a neighbor chopping wood. It felt good to be talking to my old friend, to be away from the stale smell and the dim brown light of "the cabin."

"Where they sending ya this time?" I asked.

Diet had led a disaster relief effort in Pakistan back in 2005 after an earthquake. He'd hunted for terrorists in the Philippines. He'd marched on Baghdad in 2003. Now, five years after the invasion, they were sending him back to Iraq.

"Wish I could go with you," I said.

"So come on over," he said.

That was how it all started—a dare, a halfhearted invitation that for some reason struck me like lightning. Maybe it was the casual tone of Diet's voice—maybe that's what sent me on a flight of mania, a sudden fear that I wasn't up to the challenge of an old friend, that I was a coward, that I was Eat Boy and he was Diet, and that's the way it was going to be from here on out, an ever-increasing divide between the soldier and the scribe, the fool and the warrior, real adventure and real risk a thing only one of us would ever understand, the truth of the "real world" no longer a part of my dominion, the best I could hope for being secondhand stories relayed over a cordless phone while I stared into the orange windows of a home I had no desire to call my own, my basic American craving for a new adventure a symptom of a toxic romanticism that good, intelligent people just needed to learn to lose or else sublimate into weekend warrior hobbies, harmless simulations, or perhaps daring forays into the pleasures of exotic and organic cuisine. Although it would be artificial to characterize my epiphany as something so specific as all this, I don't think it's going too far to say that the trees and the stars had something to do with the turn in the conversation, the sense of urgency I felt, the way the joke suddenly turned into a notion, a vision of two friends taking a great journey into the wild.

"What would it take to get me into Iraq?" I asked. "Hypothetically speaking."

"Hypothetically?" he said, my echo for a moment.

"Hypothetically," I said.

"Not much if you're serious," he said.

"I'm serious," I said. "I gotta get out of here."

"Ever heard of Haditha?"

"The Haditha massacre?" I said, almost eagerly, as if he'd just uttered the name of a new rollercoaster.

"Yeah," he said.

I suspect Diet was trying to veil his contempt for the way I, like much of the media, immediately connected the war—his job—to what some called "war crimes," the most violent and dramatic incidents from the conflict. But to his credit, Diet didn't immediately back down from the plot, and although it may be foolish to speculate on such things, I think I understand a few of the reasons why he was nearly as eager as I was to see where this idea would go.

Many of the folks from our hometown (Winchester, Virginia) thought of Diet as a hero, a patriot, one of the best and brightest. I believe he deserved such respect. But he was also a human being, and sometimes the more we fetishize virtue and make our friends and fellow citizens into superheroes or villains, the more we also make them less human. I think Diet loved the way some people blindly saluted the life he was living ("Thank you for your service!"), but I think he also increasingly wanted to be known. I think he wanted one of his friends to see what he was doing with his life. I think half of him was repelled by my tendencies as a writer and a liberal, but I think the other half was drawn in by our common bond of curiosity, our challenging spirits.

"We need to make this happen," I said.

"Eat Boy in Iraq," Diet said. "What a wild idea."

# 3. MARCH 2008

## IRAQ

---

The fastest way to a man's heart
is with Chuck Norris' fist.

—GRAFFITI FROM THE WAR

On the morning after my first interview with Captain Al'a, our convoy passed through the sulfuric morning breath of the Haditha dam, the sparkling crawl of the Euphrates River to our right. We saluted the marines guarding the dam. They saluted us. I didn't see a cloud in the sky as we traveled east toward a town called Barawanah, one of the three cities that make up the Haditha Triad. My map pointed out Haditha, Haqlaniyah, and Barawanah. Barawanah was known as the stronghold of the Sunni insurgents during the most vicious part of the U.S. war with Iraq. The purpose of our visit was a meeting with the police and the handoff of 12 million dinars to an Iraqi construction team that was rebuilding an all-girls school that we had bombed during the early days of the war.

I looked out my window, saw a roofless stone house atop a mound of rubble, a teal-domed minaret towering over the two-story grid of the approaching city, most of the horizontal-roofed huts and offices equipped with orange rainwater cisterns, black squiggles of Arabic graffiti silently shouting from doorways, tractors and sandbags and piles of stone everywhere. Diet, the lieutenant in charge of the JSOF (Joint Special Operations Force) unit, pointed out a power line running along the road.

"Power outages were a big problem. That was one of our projects. Not exactly what we all signed up for, more Peace Corps than SEAL, if you ask me, but whatever. We gotta clean up the mess."

"Clean up the mess" was a phrase Diet repeated probably more than any other during my weeklong visit to Haditha. When I would try to press him about his feelings on the war, he constantly returned to this notion of a "mess" that needed to be cleaned up. It was our responsibility to take care of "the mess." I don't doubt that some soldiers and politicians saw the war in Iraq as a holy struggle, a battle of good versus evil, Christianity versus Islam, or some other such reductive binary, but Diet was not one of those men, and he was careful not to ever go on the record with a direct criticism of his commander in chief. By describing the need to stay in Iraq as an obligation to "clean up the mess," he honored his men and their need for a purpose that transcended the absurd while at the same time honoring his own critical faculties. For to acknowledge a mess that needs to be cleaned up, one must therefore also acknowledge that a mess was originally made, and the story of that mess in Haditha is perhaps one of the most heartbreaking and contentious of the war.

"Baby! Baby!" screamed several children running alongside our convoy as we approached police headquarters in Barawanah.

"The marines used to throw candy," one of Diet's soldiers told me. "They think if they tell us there's a baby in the family, maybe you'll bring back the days of the candy."

I wondered if candy was the twenty-first-century equivalent of the glass beads we offered Native Americans to placate their furies. If American history remembers Haditha for anything, it'll most likely be for a day in 2005 when a platoon of marines was traveling in a convoy, much like the one I was in that March day in 2008. Everything seemed peaceful, or at least quiet, for the Third Battalion, First Marine Regiment. Maybe the marines were throwing candy to children. Maybe they were listening to some of the same music we were listening to: Rage against the Machine, Toby Keith. Maybe their lips were swollen with dip, like ours.

But then a bomb went off.

What do you do when you find yourself blown into a ditch and you can't hear and you look to your right and you look to your left, only to find the death masks of the men you were jamming out with just seconds before?

"Shoot first and ask questions later" was apparently what Staff Sgt. Frank Wuterich told his men on November 19, 2005, after an IED tore through their Humvee, splitting the vehicle in half, killing instantly a lance corporal named Miguel Terrazas.

"Shoot first and ask questions later" might be the best six-word synopsis of the Iraq War I've ever heard.

The marines stormed the city of Haditha. They killed twenty-four people. They shot teenagers and a taxi driver. They tossed grenades into homes. A nine-year-old child named Eman Waleed described the scene at his house this way: "I couldn't see their faces very well—only their guns sticking into the doorway. I watched them shoot my grandfather, first in the chest and then in the head. Then they killed my granny."

America waited until after the Iraq War was *over* to dismiss all serious charges against the marines. When anti-American sentiment returned after the bulk of American forces had left and ISIS took over in Haditha, it wasn't a surprise to me. The Haditha massacre is easy for Americans to forget, but not so much for Hadithans.

As I stepped out of the Humvee and followed Diet inside the police headquarters on that March day in 2008, I didn't feel that sense of hopelessness or anger. I was excited to meet cops and to be with a friend in whom I believed, a soldier who I knew wanted to do right. After all, one of the reasons we were there that day was to present a huge banded stack of cash as a recognition of our responsibility for the destruction of a school. Yes, we were there to clean up the mess, to build on what the news media were calling the Al Anbar Awakening, the way this entire region was starting to wake up to the righteousness of America, or something like that. I think it's important to remember this was 2008. A presidential election was right around the corner. Many people—and I was certainly one—thought the United States was about to put the era of drones and secret prisons and covert assassinations to bed. A great redeemer named Barack Obama was about to save us all.

I glanced up into the dark squares of second-floor windows on two-story buildings, looking for the muzzle of a sniper's weapon. We walked out of the sunlight and into the cool cellar smell of police headquarters, the office of one Colonel Hamid, who was dressed in green fatigues adorned with epaulettes and golden patches. Diet and Rami, my translator, introduced us. I shook the colonel's hand. He sat behind a dark wooden desk, a glass horse at the front near a golden pen set, a cabinet full of clocks and keepsakes behind him, a picture of a special unit of cops atop the cabinet, muted Iraqi music videos on the television in the corner, women tossing their hair around a man in an unbuttoned shirt, Iraqi actors expressing themselves freely. Yes, maybe life was about to become wonderful for Iraqis, the shiny happy people on TV now taunting them the way they do us.

"Salaam," we all said—the Arabic word for peace.

Captain Al'a, the mulleted leader of the SEAL-trained Iraqi SWAT team, was dressed in the same suit he had worn when I interviewed him the night before, and I could smell his Axe cologne. He sat directly to the left of the colonel, so close to his desk that he reminded me of a scolded schoolboy, the one the teacher has decided to keep close, an example for the rest. Reynolds, the public affairs officer (PAO) who had been assigned to my embed, sat, with his camera in his crotch, and to the colonel's right. I sat next to Rami and Diet against the wall on the opposite side of the room, facing a multicolored map of Iraq and the muted music videos on the cathode-ray tube TV. I was told by Rami that the mayor of Barawanah was also in the room and that he was a former human rights attorney from Baghdad. Rami nodded in the direction of a stern-faced man in a dark gray suit with no tie, prayer beads slinking through his fingers. As the conversation between Diet and the colonel began, I noticed nearly every Iraqi in the room light up a cigarette. Then, like the moment in the sitcom *Cheers*, when the obese and jovial Norm descends into the bar and is greeted by a choral incantation of his name, I heard the American soldiers all joyously cry out:

"Unis!"

I turned to my left to see a preteen tea boy in a gray dishdasha blushing and smiling as he carried a tray of tiny cups. The collective smiles made me smile. The laughs made me laugh. The colonel seemed confused by this spontaneous yet coordinated explosion of affection for young Unis. The colonel waited for the noise to die down before attending to business.

"We've had no insurgent attacks since July," he said, looking directly toward me, as if he were reporting to me. Like the diligent pupil, I took out my journal and jotted down notes. I nodded with the gravitas of an anchorman.

"We've shut down thirteen cells," Captain Al'a added, according to Rami. Al'a then described at length a weapons cache that he and his men had discovered and destroyed just that week. Photographs of cartridges and wires were passed around the room. I started to feel like I was at a pep rally, like maybe that was the entire point of an embed—a grand show-and-tell for soldiers and cops and ultimately for everyone in America.

Of course the flip side of this feeling is that it shows just how deeply and instinctively most media personnel mistrust good news. Sometimes things do change. Sometimes things get better. See the abolition of slavery, the defeat of Hitler, the eradication of leprosy and polio and the recent development of an Ebola vaccine. Maybe, I kept telling myself, there is a story here that is both uplifting and true. I wanted so badly to believe that the catastrophe in Iraq was coming to an end and that my friend was instrumental to this happy ending, this mopped-up mess.

"But what about them?" my father had asked just before I left. "Who's their good guy? Who's their George Washington? That's the story you want to find. Talk to *them*."

How 'bout this guy in the mullet, Dad? Was it possible that I could have my cake and eat it too? Was it possible that I was in the presence of the perfect Iraq war story, a balance of redneck jingoism and *Daily Show* absurdity, the Iraqi redeemer as this mulleted SWAT team leader who had been trained by a hometown hero here in the heart of darkness, this city of the most infamous massacre in the war? Look, Dad, he's using American cash to shut down cells left and right. Look, America, the dollar diplomacy we liked to call the Al Anbar Awakening was working. Just look at the way the money is bringing together the colonel, the captain, the Iraqis, and the Americans.

God, I tried so hard to believe, and it wasn't just for my father. My mother, like my father, was an optimist, a mischievous, bright-eyed woman from the Midwest (Zanesville, Ohio) who didn't like to see me fight with my father about America. My brother and sister usually kept to the sidelines when it came to dinner-table debates about politics, and our conversations weren't usually even worthy of the term "debate" until after the invasion of Iraq. I didn't like feeling alienated from my father and his patriotism, so I think it was his hope that his wisdom about finding Iraq's George Washington might just help close the gap between us insofar as a George Washington from Iraq was still a sincere testament to the powerful revolutionary example of the founding father of the United States.

After the meeting with the colonel I followed the example of the Iraqis and squatted down into a catcher's crouch on the edge of a stony stall where we all shared a gray bar of soap before lunch. A knee-high spigot streamed cool water, and Captain Al'a and one of his men joined us just as the soap broke in my hand. It felt like a moment of communion when I gave them each a piece of the soap they had given me.

As we walked down a half-lit hallway, I thought about the meeting, how all the cops waited an hour before bringing up the recent crimes, a kidnapping of three Iraqi travelers thirty miles to the northeast along a desert highway known as Baje Road. How much of the conversation I had just witnessed was "cleansed?" I wanted to ask Captain Al'a this question in this rare moment alone, but my translator had already washed his hands and I could see him standing against a mud brick wall with Diet as we emerged onto a bright courtyard, a fenced-in cloister in the rear of the compound where a long banquet table of silver, shield-sized plates sat piled with white rice and stewed beans, large bony chunks of goat, a layer of naan bread beneath each heap.

The Iraqis stood off to the side with their hands behind their backs.

"Shukran," I said, using the Arabic for "thank you."

And then the "goat grab" began. I followed Diet's lead, digging in with my right hand. I licked my fingers, tasted the residue of that communal bar of gray soap, wondered for a moment if I was on the edge of some life-changing bacterial invasion, my journey to Iraq about to be cut short by a bout of explosive, never-ending diarrhea. Damn. Why does this always happen to me? I had to pinch myself continuously to keep from laughing as I imagined the bodies of all these uniformed men buckling and shuddering, hands reaching for the heavens as their bowels betrayed them, mullets aflutter, mustaches beaded with sweat, Americans and Iraqis unified in a ballet of bowel movements.

"Hi-zeyn," I said, Arabic for "it is good."

Captain Al'a gave a big appreciative smile as he folded a white cloth napkin in his hands. He seemed thrilled by the fact that I knew a few phrases, that I was trying. Rami unzipped his jumpsuit just a bit. I watched Diet speaking with the police, the young members of his Iraqi SWAT team. I was nearly tearful with pride. They listened to Diet, my friend. They liked him. They seemed to admire his candor and humor, just as I did. He made a trundling motion with his hand as he described our child-hood town in Virginia. He told them Winchester was a lot like Haditha, a hundred miles or so from the capital, lots of open land for young men to get into mischief.

"This is where the trouble happens," he said.

The cops nodded with mirthful, cheek-swollen faces, perhaps remem-bering for a moment when they too were boys at play. But try to imagine this one crucial difference between Haditha and Winchester, Virginia, where Diet and I grew up: in 2008 the unemployment rate in Haditha was 70 percent. Imagine how American men would behave in an econ-omy like that. Look at the sense of listlessness and anger we see now, in 2019, as we hover around 5 percent unemployment. Double that. Double it again. And again. And again. People tend to see terrorism in the con-text of some geopolitical chess match, or perhaps as a war of religions or ideologies. But follow the yellow brick road. Where do we find wealthy countries with single-digit unemployment ripped in half by rebellion? Sitting here in the year 2019, little more than a year after the race riot in Charlottesville, I ask that rhetorical question with more than just a little nervousness.

After lunch, just before we visited the girls' school U.S. forces had bombed back in 2005, Diet and I stepped into a municipal building down the street to meet with the mayor of Barawanah. His name was Myasah Almahsin. He shook my hand and invited me into an office where I saw billowing champagne-colored curtains, a modern colored map of Iraq next to a parchment counterpart in the far corner. A small white refrigerator with an image of a green apple magnetized in the center sat within reach of the mayor's desk. By the door was a tall wooden cabinet loaded with binders, photos of a large extended family framed on the top shelf.

"Candy?"

The mayor offered me a caramel, a "mella." He smiled at my appreciative moans as I savored the sweet. He pushed the bag across his desk, told me I could take them all. I didn't refuse. I put the bag in my pocket.

"Eat Boy," Diet said, disclosing my high school nickname.

"What?"

Diet shook his head. Rami laughed. I wasn't exactly sure what to ask the mayor. I was eager to see the school we had destroyed. The mayor, having been a human rights attorney from Baghdad, was probably a devoted public servant, more than just a functionary, more than just a bureaucrat with binders. But I'm not going to sit here and lie. I didn't want to see inside his binders. I didn't want to have a conversation about human rights. I was hungry for drama. I wanted to see the disaster site and hear more about the massacre. I asked perfunctory questions for a while and thus received perfunctory answers. I popped another "mella," felt like here was the real information, this sweet taste, and, for a certain kind of writer, this of course is the thing—this moment. We know through candy and tea and dripping chunks of meat and the cool, calming fizz of a Coke or a Pepsi that the man across the table from us is a man, just like us. We know when he lifts his leg to release a silent fart that he too is a human being, not some subhuman variable in a polemic. This man who loves candy is not a "high-value target" or an "asset" or just some "crazy Muslim." No, he is an Iraqi human being and maybe he has children and a wife, and maybe he too has a mother who is sick and was once a teacher, and maybe he too has a father with high hopes and a sister who worries about him and a brother to whom he's always trying to prove himself, and maybe he too has doubts about America and look at that subtle savoring smile as he sucks on his postprandial sweet. About a half hour into my interview, this basic but crucial candy-inspired epiphany came into me like a timed-release powder from a pill.

Somehow the perfunctory mood passed, as if my father were whispering in my ear, "What about them?" I asked the mayor about the children at the school, how war had changed their lives. Just the thought of them—the children—and the fact that I hadn't been thinking about them up until this point—nearly made me cry. The mayor came to life, wheeled away from his desk, scooted forward in his seat. He began to talk about the families of his city and the unintended consequences of war. Children no longer at school are now children at home, which is a burden on the mother. Suddenly, the father does not have a job because of the war and the mother can only do half of what she could do before because she must now watch the children. The mother grows stressed. She takes medicine, the American pills. Antidepressants, with their world of side effects, unintended consequences. The mayor swung his arms like an air traffic controller.

"And then there are the textbooks from Jordan," he said. "Our government no longer dictates the contents of the textbooks for the children, and this is good, right?"

The mayor was on a roll. I looked up at Diet for approval, as if to make sure we were still on the same team. He was stone faced, appropriately inscrutable. The Navy SEAL.

"Think about our history with Iran," the mayor said. "Iran is the devil, right? The Shiite devil to the east. This was the story in the old textbooks. But one of the unintended consequences of liberation has been the liberation of history. Our children now see from the American textbooks that we receive from Jordan that Iran is not the devil and that maybe we, Iraqis, have more in common with Iranians than we thought and that maybe they could be our friends."

Diet shook his head as Rami translated this last bit. I was not the only one suffering from naivete. This textbook revelation was not good news for George W. Bush and Dick Cheney and their vision of an "axis of evil." The American invasion was—unintentionally—convincing Iraqis that Iranians were human beings, creatures who liked candy and family and whose history was riddled with meddling and, who knows, just might be able to be trusted as friends, neighbors. Here is the fundamental danger of history: empathy. What if we all start thinking of everyone as human beings? What would happen to defense budgets?

"Time to go," Diet said.

I suddenly wished I'd had more time with the mayor. I felt I was on the edge of a big story I can only now begin to see. Perhaps this moment in Mayor Almahsin's office was the first time I began to think of the Global War on Terror in terms of its impact on global literacy, the way children in Iraq viewed their neighbors in Iran, and the way that perception is facilitated by American policy. How did the Global War on Terror transform the educational practices of schools in Iraq, Afghanistan, Mali, Kenya, Indonesia, Texas, and Pakistan? To what degree did the Iraqi refugee crisis that followed the American invasion lead to an invasion of classrooms and study groups? To what extent did our delivery of the internet deliver the means for Iraqis to read America through the new lenses of social media and the perspectives of their neighbors?

I thanked the mayor for his candy, returned to our Humvee, felt wide awake from that conversation as we slowly rolled through the streets past the stares of shopkeepers and their sons, boys on bikes, roofless recently destroyed homes left and right, sudden grassy groves of date palms, women reading to children in the shade. I took out my camera, captured hostile faces from a trio of Iraqi women in black abayas and white hijabs, their children in hand-me-down, cartoon-covered American apparel, and then, marching out of an alley like a mafia hit squad, stepped four of the largest Middle Eastern women I'd ever seen, one of them with an abaya inflated to proportions that defied the parameters of a pregnancy.

But that woman did not blow herself up, and I do not know why her obesity remains such a mystery to me to this day. We parked in front of a small market, real live Iraqi human beings everywhere with their thinness and obesity, their fruits and vegetables and Iraqi soda and Iraqi candy and American shirts. I looked for another bag of the caramels I'd scored from the mayor, something I could take home as a souvenir for my brother and sister, who both loved soccer and exotic wooden sculptures and masks. But I didn't see any jerseys or masks, and, besides, there was no time for shopping. We moved quickly inside an iron gate.

The world grew quiet. A soft warm wind skittered sand across the ground and over my face. I found myself in a courtyard surrounded by rows of empty desks under a depthless azure sky, a hive of caves forming a crescent behind the whitewashed walls of this empty school. A basketball hoop stood like a tall awkward teenager in the middle of it all.

"See those holes up there?" Diet said.

I followed his finger into the crumbly crescent sandstone wall, where I could see several cats sleeping in front of the doorways that recessed into the caves.

"What do you do if you've got insurgents hiding in caves behind a school?"

A man in a black jacket and a dark blue dress shirt, accompanied by a short man in a gray dishdasha, greeted us in the center of the courtyard. We all shook hands and said "the peace be upon you" and then moved around into the small, empty classrooms. For a moment I took my helmet off and ran my hand through my hair, which had grown longer than I'd allowed it to in years. I felt good and awake, proud to be part of this team that was taking responsibility for the mess the United States had made. As we walked upstairs and moved atop the roof, I saw faces in distant second-story windows. I put my helmet back on. I stood under the shade of magnificent palm trees, climbed as high as I could to see into the caves—this primitive space we've come to associate with the evil of the Arabic-speaking world. It is the cave where the terrorists like Bin Laden hide out and plot America's doom. But maybe these cave dwellers who use children as shields and huddle with guns near a school or a mosque are really just your run-of-the mill human beings, the kind who like candy and want to live, the kind who maybe believe that there's still such a thing as a rule, a home base, a place where you can call "olly olly oxen free," a white-flag zone of peace and rest. But this was the Global War on Terror, what Dick Cheney called "the dark side." For both Iraqis and Americans, those Geneva Convention days were done. Was peace possible after the lines both sides had crossed?

From atop the roof I watched my friend stand beneath a corrugated shelter precariously held up by knobby poles, the sawed-off trunks of trees. I saw dusty bags of cement stacked everywhere, a few children walking cautiously into the scene. Reynolds, my PAO, clipped pictures with his big black Canon, and so did I, with my tiny silver Kodak. We drifted back and forth between the conversation down below, the handoff of cash, and the mystery of these caves in front of us, the snoozing white cat and the ragged red-and-blue cloth doorway suggesting someone was hiding—or maybe just living—inside these spaces once again. It struck me like thunder that maybe it's possible that people who live in caves just live there. Maybe they're not hiding or building IEDs. Maybe they're just living in the landscape instead of flattening it to build boxes.

We walked back downstairs to witness the handoff of the cash, the sons of the man in the gray dishdasha watching us with curiosity, the youngest among them named Faris. Diet gave him a Jolly Rancher. The child smiled. He wore a long-sleeve white-and-gray polo shirt with a bright blue undershirt and a bright red shirt beneath that, his layers of clothing giving him the illusion of thickness. As his father talked business with Diet, I knelt down and asked him for a high five. He understood. We slapped hands. I told him to go low, and when I pulled my hand away and said "too slow," he seemed heartbroken, absolutely devastated. So I gave him a second chance. He nailed it this time.

"Want a picture?"

I looked up and saw Reynolds smiling and squinting in the sun. I gave him my camera. I was not at all aware that the photo we were about to take was a dangerous and saccharine statement, a sentimental "white savior" shot taken on the edge of a bombed-out school with a child who probably had no clue about the history of his country and therefore couldn't rightfully represent the story of the Iraq War. But maybe history is just as much about forgetting as it is remembering, one always leading to the other, the innocent actor always precursor to the memorable act, the boy always preface to the man. I put my arm around Faris, the rows of empty desks under the sun behind our backs. We both beamed for the camera. As of that day, I had never even heard the term "white savior." Upon seeing our smiles in the photo, I didn't think about the mysterious role of privilege or race in this image and the histories of this war certain people will write. I simply thought, *This will be a good shot for the folks back home who still believe in peace.*

# 4. NOVEMBER 2007

## AMERICA

The enemy is in the White House.

Not over here.

—GRAFFITI FROM THE WAR

Eager to share the news of my upcoming journey to Iraq, I drove toward a restaurant near my brother's home in Chapel Hill, North Carolina. Chapel Hill may well be the southern headquarters for liberal academic consciousness, one of those places where in 2007 the antiwar sentiment was, if not strong, at least present. Passing through the suburbs, one would often see peace signs in the front yards of homes, bumper stickers that said things like, "When Jesus said love your enemy, I think he meant don't kill them."

My brother, Andy, was a research oncologist at Duke University. Sometimes I felt inferior to Andy. Whenever we'd get together, I always felt like I had to prove myself to him and our parents. I suppose I was afraid they all saw me as the man I might just become: an irrelevant dilettante who was willing to sacrifice a meaningful engagement with the world for the narcissistic pleasures of escapist fiction and indie rock 'n' roll. I'd just turned thirty that summer. I'd just called off my engagement. I'd never once sold a story, but I believed with a delusional vigor that I was meant to be a writer. Thus, as my family sat at a pizza parlor in a mini-mall off Weaver Dairy Road, I thought it was important to cut off the inevitable questions about my life, or lack thereof, and make a preemptive attack—tell the family right away about this incredibly meaningful thing I was about to do.

"Hey, Dad, guess what?" I said. "I'm going to Iraq."

I was sitting at the end of the table across from my father and mother, my father's face Scottish red, his hair silver, my mother's hair all grown back that fall, but thinner than it had been in the past. She was in remission. This was reason enough to be happy, perhaps the underlying impetus for the minireunion: a chance to savor each other's company while we still could, my mother's cancer a strange blessing upon our family insofar as it made us realize how precious our time together would be. Of course the other side of that blessing, that sense of knowing that one's time is limited, is a feeling of urgency about other things. When was the next time a Navy SEAL would invite me to the heart of a war?

At the other end of the table that night were my brother and his children and my sister-in-law. Then, closer to us, in the middle, sat Andy's wife's father, Bob. Bob was a nuclear physicist for the Naval Research Center. Bob had a sad but wise Italian face. I looked into his eyes to see if I'd captured his interest with my announcement, perhaps a flicker of respect from a man who truly knew something about WMDs. I looked for the same out of my parents. I wanted them to lace their fingers together and hunch forward and ask me penetrating questions about my "mission." I wanted them to feel what I felt: adrenaline, curiosity, self-righteous anger, the fatigue of witnessing war from the sidelines suddenly replaced with the possibility of seeing the thing for ourselves, one of their own about to investigate the great plague of our time—the war in Iraq.

So why weren't their faces lighting up? Why wasn't the warm glow of the pizza parlor spotlight shining down on me as the pizzas arrived at the table? Bob the nuclear physicist did something funny with his eyes, a squinty, fart-stifling face of disapprobation.

"You're doing what?" he said.

"He's not going to Iraq," my mother said. "He's just joking."

My father smiled sheepishly, believing, I think, that I was indeed joking. After all, I wasn't a journalist, and that—being the joker—was my real role in the family as well as among my friends. Although it was true that I'd always harbored a real interest in the secret history of the

United States and that I'd taken the time to memorize all the presidents in chronological order as a child, my true voice in the family was that of the trickster or the prankster, the kid who was always doing voices and farting and trying to place his sleeping brother's hand in a bucket of warm water so brother would wet the bed and thus come down a peg closer to the earth.

"I'm not kidding," I said. "I'm going. I talked to Diet the other night. We're going to make it happen. I'm going to get the *Winchester Star* to sponsor me."

This was the first anyone had heard of the *Winchester Star*'s involvement, and by "anyone," I mean to include myself. The *Winchester Star* was our hometown newspaper, and although it was true that I hadn't acquired sponsorship, I hadn't exactly told my parents that I had. What I told them was, "I'm going to get the *Winchester Star* to sponsor me." And no sooner were those words out of my mouth than I believed them. But nobody seemed to care. Bob started eating pizza and talking to the grandchildren. My mother still seemed to think I was joking. My father, however, was another story. He seemed to feel my sincerity. I could see it in his eyes, the reddening of his already florid face.

"You know, I have a patient whose daughter is a missionary in Lebanon. If you want to see the Mideast, that would be safer. I could talk to him."

"Dad, I don't want to go to Lebanon."

"You're not a journalist," he said. "How are you going to get over there?"

"The *Winchester Star*," I said.

"You're not going to Iraq," he said.

But my father was wrong. As a child, I experienced many times when I attended camp and it didn't appeal to me or I didn't like a team I was on or a school I was attending. And there were several moments in particular when my father took me aside and dressed me down for my persistent thoughts of quitting.

"You are not a quitter," he would always say. "You are not going to quit."

But I was a quitter for a long time, or if I wasn't, I knew the quitter was a strong force battling inside of me; after all, I had recently called off my engagement, my plans to start a nuclear family. That was a big thing to quit, and in a way it was a rebuke not just of my own hypothetical family but perhaps domesticity in general. If I was going to quit Karen, what was I quitting her and our hypothetical family for? It certainly wasn't another woman, and it wasn't a man. If there's one thing I've felt extreme passion for in my life—if I've had one secret mistress—it's been this thing in front of you, this conversation right here, and I'm talking about something bigger than just "writing," and the word *politics* just doesn't do the hunger proper justice and neither does the word *prankster* or *joker* or *trickster*.

Shortly after that dinner in November, a lakelike calm descended on me, a feeling of purpose, like Rocky Balboa in those training montages as he's getting ready to fight the Russian or Mr. T or Apollo Creed. After a number of rejections and no-responses from big newspapers in Virginia and North Carolina, I returned to the idea of my hometown paper, the *Winchester Star*. I was familiar with the newspaper's editor, Tom Byrd. He was the uncle of an old grade-school classmate of mine, Gretchen, whom I emailed. I called home and talked to my mother, who cackled her wonderful cackle when I mentioned his name because my mother knew that Tom Byrd and I saw the world in very different ways. She told me that Byrd was a conservative like his father, Harry Byrd Jr., the former senator, so if I was going to try to sell him on an embed, my mother said, "keep your opinions close to your vest." My mother was a liberal and an activist. She once led a grassroots campaign to keep a very irresponsible corporation from setting up shop near the banks of the Shenandoah River, much to the chagrin of the Winchester business community and perhaps Tom Byrd himself. My mother knew the political lay of the land in our hometown. So I took her advice.

On November 22, 2007, after Byrd received my first letter, in which I told him I wished to tell the story of a young lieutenant from our hometown who was serving as a Navy SEAL in the heart of Al Anbar Province, Byrd replied.

Matt:
Thanks for the information. I will study and respond Monday.
Best wishes and thanks for thinking of the *Winchester Star*.
Tom

Three days later came his answer.

Matt:

Yes, the *Winchester Star* is interested in sponsoring you for a tour in Iraq. What are the steps to take and what is our cost?

Tom

I couldn't believe it. I was terrified. I was jubilant. I wrote to Diet. I started the official paperwork with the military's media relations office. I provided my name, date of birth, and my area of interest. I said I wanted to embed with the SEAL platoon stationed in Haditha and that my sponsor was the *Winchester Star*. I called my brother. I called my parents. There was nothing I loved more than sharing a triumph with my mother and father.

The night that I received the email from Byrd, I emerged from my bedroom and found Joe on the couch with his laptop, his white cat, Siggy, perched near his shoulder.

"I'm going to Iraq!" I said. "I just heard back from my hometown newspaper. They're going to pay for everything."

"Really?" Joe said. "Just like that?"

I smiled. I felt vindicated, as if I had discovered that fortune was just waiting to favor the bold. Two days later, on Wednesday, Joe and I packed up our gear for band practice, and between songs over the microphone Joe announced my intentions. Our drummer, Sean, a gigantic man we sometimes called Big Daddy, seemed genuinely happy for me.

"Matty!" he said. "Shit! I want to go!"

We practiced in a little boxcar-sized shed in Sean's backyard. We often played with Spike, Sean's pit bull, between sets. At one point that night, with our ears ringing and Spike running rabid laps around the backyard, I suddenly took to chasing him, driving him wild with the special attention of a feverish pursuit. I felt young and alive, like I could run all night. That shed—my job, my home, my broken engagement—these things all seemed signs of a sideways life prior to that letter from Byrd, evidence of a life on hold, a "failure to launch," a man who'd reached a plateau. But that night, chasing that white blur around the backyard under the stars, I felt like everything was about to change.

Shortly after I got the word from Tom Byrd about the *Winchester Star* sponsoring my trip to Iraq, I received a phone call from Diet alerting me to the fact that my father had been calling his father in an attempt to convince him—Diet's father—to convince Diet to convince me not to go to Iraq. I was furious when I heard about it, embarrassed to be chastised by my old boyhood friend like I was some kind of fool.

"Eat Boy," Diet said. "You're a man. This is your decision. If you come over here, you're going to be with a platoon of Navy SEALs. Your dad thinks you're going to get your head chopped off, and he wants me to tell you that shit like that happens, and yeah, shit like that happens, but look who it happens to. That does not happen to SEALs."

I did not like being talked to like that. Just as I had an inferiority complex when it came to my brother, I also had one when it came to Diet. Diet and my brother lived in the land of the body. They slaughtered and saved real human bodies. I, meanwhile, played with and pursued the paths of the mind and did not yet have a yogi in my mind to remind me that the mind was part of the body. No, I did not like learning of my father's meddling from the man in my group of friends who had always acted like my father.

This is probably a good place to share a little more about this father figure we're both agreeing to call Diet in the name of honoring national security. Growing up, Diet was a blond-haired boy, a third-generation German whose parents divorced when we were in grade school. As far back as I can remember, he was always getting up early for swim team practice, often arriving at school having been awake for three to four hours longer than I. He was known as the "virgin buster" in high school. His increasingly long hair, perhaps on account of so much chlorine, was so woolly that a friend once said to him in the cafeteria, "Diet, you got that kind hair. Kind that grows out of a dog's ass."

The military took care of his "kind" hair. Two years before he went to Annapolis, here's how he got the nickname Diet: One of our favorite spots to backpack was an old World War II training camp in West Virginia known as Dolly Sods. Once, in the summer, while walking down a trail, the six of us who were hiking on that trip decided to set up teams of two so we could wage petty battles with each other. For example, if one guy from one team could get another guy from another team to say "What?" after calling out his name, and then thwart that man's curiosity by offering nothing in response, well, that man would then register a point for his team. Hiding a crayfish in someone's water bottle could also win you points. Long story short—Diet, before he was known as Diet, was losing points on that trip to Dolly Sods by virtue of his teammate, Grover. During that particular summer trip, someone remarked on how sloppy Grover's backpack was packed, the way it resembled an old jalopy, straps and wires and frayed cloth zigzagging everywhere, water bottles and carabiners jangling off the sides, tent poles slipping out of their sockets every few minutes or so to the point that someone couldn't help but compare Grover's pack to the tightly cinched aerodynamic vessel on his partner's back, and therefore that someone told Grover that his pack needed to go on a diet. Thus, for a brief period of time on that trip, there was Grover, and there was Diet Grover. After that trip was over, Diet Grover's name was shortened to Diet.

My nickname, Eat Boy, was given to me when I was fifteen and couldn't drive and was catching a ride to lunch one day with the pre-Diet Diet in his black Subaru Brat, those old late-eighties vehicles that seemed a cross between a sedan and a cheap truck. Sitting outside of Enrico's Pizza just a few blocks down the road from the town's neoclassical bell tower, which country high school boys like us sometimes vandalized, I munched away on a meatball sub, thrilled to be out on the town when most other kids were eating Salisbury steaks back in the school cafeteria. My unconscious delight suddenly turned into self-conscious shame, however, when one of my meatballs popped out and went skidding down the gray upholstery of the Brat, leaving a red marinara path that dropped off where the meatball went tumbling toward the floor. Diet cursed. Repeatedly. This was not the first time I'd made a mess. I suppose I was known for it—making messes.

"Fucking Eat Boy," Diet said, out of nowhere, and thus the name was born, and it was christened later that week when Diet presented me with a clipping of a Campbell's Soup ad showing the round-faced kid-character in a logoless ball cap slamming home a spoonful of savory broth. I stuck that picture in my high school locker and still have it to this day, stowed away in a lockbox with my favorite baseball cards because it was given to me by Diet, a man whom I have always admired like a father.

As time went on, I think we both realized to some degree that there was a collective identity here and maybe even an inkling that identity meant nothing outside of the collective, that seemingly simple social notion that you can't have one without the other. I, Eat Boy, was to embrace the mess of life, the chaos, the spider's web, the goo of psychedelic consciousness, the unpredictable sexually promiscuous women most men would be afraid to bring home to their folks, the strange life a glutton comes to know at the far outreaches of gluttony, the Blakean wisdom-slash-delusion of the fool following his folly to excess.

Diet, on the other hand, took the straight road, the one many of our friends mocked in the nineties, the path of memorized reef points, epaulets, swabbing the deck and reaming the hull, the old rip-cord line he loved to utter when parents would ask him about the Naval Academy while the rest of us were having the time of our life.

"It's a bad place to be but a good place to come from," he'd say, and the parents would nod knowingly, and we'd all make rip-cord motions behind his back and restrain laughter when he'd appear in his starched whites, and why? Because *he* was suddenly different. Diet was now the Other. The stranger. By taking the path of sameness, conformity, uniform, and service, Diet was doing something most folks in my draft-free generation just couldn't bring themselves to do: serve, submit, surrender to the collective, the socialist machine of the military. The truth is, Diet wasn't really conforming or taking the straight, easy road. After the twin towers went down, he found himself staring down one hell of a mess while the rest of us at home did everything in our power to pretend like we had nothing to do with that mess.

That history.

Now, here he was sharing the story of my father's meddling and reminding me in a new way of everything I was not. Furious, I hung up the phone, paced around in the brown darkness of that Colfax kitchen, the tall black trees in the backyard towering over the house and shedding their leaves in the wind. I stepped outside onto the deck to look up at the stars and clear my head. The will to go to Iraq deepened against my father's opposition, his willingness to meddle. Not to mention Diet's challenge.

"Eat Boy, you're a man."

Several days later, I nearly exploded after receiving a call from Tom Byrd, editor of the newspaper.

"I'm sorry, Matt," he said. "But we're not going to be able to sponsor a trip to Iraq."

"What?" I said.

What the hell had happened? I stood up from the bristly blue couch and began to pace and shake. Byrd said he'd had time to think about it, and in spite of his commitment via email, he now didn't believe I had the proper training to enter a war zone. I argued with him, essentially making the point that every journalist in a war zone was at one time a journalist who had never entered a war zone. There has to be a first time. I was locked in a catch-22. I reiterated my conviction that Diet's story was a good one and that it was made for the *Winchester Star*. But there was no convincing Tom Byrd. Something had changed his mind.

"Matt, I'm sorry," he said.

He hung up. I continued to pace and shake. Joe wasn't home. It was just me and the animals and the computer, the sun going down, no cable TV, the world suddenly seeming so fucking cowardly and impenetrable, a fortress of fear. I felt baffled and thwarted. I felt frustrated. I felt like I'd done something wrong but couldn't name it. I felt like a loser. I was trying my best to get out of my room and into the world, into the center of events, where I might be able to see something and therefore say something or maybe even *do* something of value. But it was hard to escape the room, that house we called "the cabin." The world seemed to be conspiring to keep me locked up in that remote rural outpost, and as a writer who studied the lives of other writers, I knew there was a mixed message in this fear I was facing. One perspective suggests it is the writer's job to stay in the room, to not yield to the geographical cure, the grasping and groping that comes from following the Hemingway and Kerouac spirit, that intuitive sense that the story and the truth are *out there*. Be this as it may, I loved Hemingway and Kerouac and others, like Jack London. I valued the fruits of their sacrifice. And as Hemingway once wrote, "War is the best subject of all."

"War hath determined us," Milton writes in *Paradise Lost*, but I felt like war was determined to avoid me. I wanted to see my generation's war. I wanted to see the damn thing that was shaping everything else. I paced my way into the night, a feeling beginning to grow inside of me. I don't know if I began to fear my father's secret hand in these events that night, but I do remember my mind racing, my body thrashing around in bed. I tried to use booze and porn to kill the feeling, but it didn't work.

Later that week I sat in a dark classroom with my students and listened to a librarian talk to us about the importance of careful research. Caffeine was the only thing keeping me from a sense of despair during those daytime hours in which my engagement with my students was usually enough human interaction to prevent me from feeling utterly rudderless and isolated. But since it was that time of the year when the librarians were charged with taking over a week of our introductory writing courses, I suddenly found myself without the sanctuary of those human moments, that precious conversation with students. Sitting in that basement room of North Carolina A&T's Bluford Library, watching my students sleep and text while a kind but out-of-touch white librarian tried to engage them with jokes about movies from the eighties, I had no idea that I was experiencing boredom in the same quarters that the mastermind of 9/11 had experienced boredom two decades earlier. I tried to find a way out of the feeling. Full of caffeine and frustration, I wondered if maybe I'd made a tremendous mistake by backing out on marriage and children, by banking on writing above all else, by seeing writing as this transcendent enterprise. I began to think of Karen and our old house and the dogs and all the good times we'd had, how maybe I'd been a coward to leave it all behind, and how maybe it still wasn't too late to go back.

Maybe Thomas Wolfe was wrong.

*Maybe you can go home again. Maybe your father is right and is doing what he can to steer you back to the golden road before it's too late, Matt. Maybe you're lost. Maybe it is November and your despair over your mother's sickness and the love that you've lost has taken you to a pale*

*rim of a placeless place where you've never been before, and maybe your*
*father also feels this November feeling but knows it better than you from*
*the years of Novembers he's known. Maybe you really would've gotten*
*your head chopped off if you'd gone to Iraq. Maybe you truly are lost. But*
*maybe it's not too late.*

These voices were growing stronger. And that day, those voices won. I
drove past our old house. No. I did not drive past. I stopped. Karen wasn't
there and neither was the mysterious Jeep Cherokee. I let Evildoer lick
my hand through the fence for good luck. I drove down Battleground
Avenue to Gold's Gym, where Karen and I used to work out. I didn't know
what I was doing, but when I saw Karen's silver Prius, I knew I had to do
something. I marched into the gym and the smell of sweat and metal,
the sound of supplements grinding down in a blender. I saw the TVs and
treadmills and spandex and free weights everywhere, old music videos
playing on the central screen banks, the evening news above the cardio
machines against the far wall, where I'd occasionally see Karen in my
old Baltimore Orioles cap, jogging away her stress. But she wasn't there.
I felt frantic, like a cross between a maniac and one of those zany heroes
from the romantic comedies of the eighties, Crocodile Dundee searching
through the million faces of strangers in New York City so he can recon-
cile with his American lover, and of course the honest apology is always
warmly welcomed in such movies and always eloquently delivered and
backed up by buoying notes from a booming soundtrack, the struggling
couple left kissing in the center of the cheering masses as the credits roll,
redemption always there if you just have the courage to tell the truth
and speak your heart like Crocodile Dundee.

But what if you don't know the truth of your heart? Did I truly want
to get back together with my ex or was I just lonely and desperate, my
rejection by the *Winchester Star* the equivalent of a rebuff from a beautiful mistress sending the reeling, unfaithful husband back home to his
henpecking wife with a dozen red roses and a box of chocolates and a
million promises for a fresh start and another baby?

I passed by TVs showing scenes from the war, Code Orange all over
Fox News. I pressed my face against the glass of the five o'clock aerobics
class, and there, among the reaching and kicking and jumping bodies,

was Karen. I watched her move, felt a hunger for her touch, her smile. She was wearing that Orioles hat, which seemed a good omen. She turned around at one point and I waved to her. She offered me a quizzical look in exchange. I made a trundling motion with my hand, felt like a mime, a man in prison, or some kind of awful hellish mute dream where you're locked away from the faces of your life. I wanted her to step outside that room so I could tell her how much I loved her, but beneath all the lines I wanted to utter was a growing nervousness, a fear that I was just dealing with a feeling and not really dealing at all. Yielding—that's all I was doing. I was just like a flag or a plastic bag, a piece of loose garbage blowing in the wind. And I half knew it, but I wanted to seem like a man, so instead of owning up to the conflicted feeling, I put on a strong and certain voice, and I tried to stick with it, but out in the parking lot in front of Gold's Gym with the logo of a muscle-bound man looking down from the cheap plaster walls of that mini-mall plaza—I began to cry.

Karen came outside. We sat down in the parking lot under a paling sky of emerging stars and inland gulls, people getting their dinner from the drive-thru at the Wendy's behind us. When I said "I miss you," I meant it. That much was true. And when her eyes filled with tears, I knew she missed me, too. Sometimes you can miss somebody so much that you create another person in their absence, a ghost, and thus you totally miss who they were by virtue of having replaced them with who you want them to be. I knew I was doing that even as I told her that everything was all my fault. Even as I was sitting there on a concrete parking block with my fists shaking at the sky begging for her to come back, I was remembering just how tense and awful the last year of our relationship had been, her fist busting through the glass of our bedroom window, me always on drives late at night, sleeping in hotels just to breathe. After an hour of stuttering confessions and stillborn pleas, as it became clear to me that she wasn't going to take me back, I actually began to feel relieved. My apology had served some ejaculatory purpose that had more to do with me than Karen.

Maybe one of the toughest parts about being an American man is living in a country that worships strong and silent military men (superheroes) on the screen and at the same time learning to own up to just how complicated your emotions can be, acknowledging that you're sometimes more than just blowjobs, farts, and touchdowns—and sometimes less. The real man can speak of this, these moments of levity and failure, what's going on down below. The boy instead continues with his script of certitude, his love that is so strong that only a war can cure it.

"Sometimes I feel like I just want to die," I said to Karen. "I'm thinking about going to Iraq."

# 5. MARCH 2008

## IRAQ

Chuck Norris needs one roll of TP
per shit.
—GRAFFITI FROM THE WAR

I wanted to swim the Euphrates. Even though I had been told by Diet that it wasn't safe to swim in the river, I didn't get antsy about the implications of such warnings when I would stand on the river's edge and look into the dark water blasted out of the Haditha dam. Then one morning that changed when I took my translator, Rami, up on his offer to show me the other side of the river.

Accompanied by Reynolds, Rami and I climbed the steps to the top of the dam. It was a warm morning. The Soviet concrete of this Iraqi dam appeared functional and opaque, a narrowly vented trapezoid. Clouds hovered over the hamlets in the distance like ghostly regattas, their shapes burning off above the Al Jazira desert, where we were scheduled to go on a hunt for Al Qaeda the next day. Would we find them? Was this the last day of my life? When we reached the top of the dam, I took off my orange Capilene shirt and asked Reynolds to take a picture of me. It felt good to feel the desert sun on my chest and to laugh about getting a tan here on my spring break in Iraq.

Ten stories tall and a football field wide with gigantic concrete wings on both sides, the dam at times appeared to me as a kind of stone beast, a sleeping, multieyed leviathan that would occasionally belch out its waters to the peasants in the distance. We walked around the top for a moment, threaded our way through what looked to be abandoned concrete toll-booths decorated with Arabic graffiti. These were the old surveillance posts for the Iraqi army. Reynolds talked about his life, how Haditha had been a "hornets' nest" at the beginning of the war, and how he had been part of the early air force forays into Afghanistan. He mentioned how close we were to the border, to the thousands of refugees who had left Iraq and were now living just next door in Syria. Reynolds was a Mormon, a farrier, a bull rider with a bull's hoofprint scarred into the middle of his forehead. Diet and his fellow SEALs spoke of Reynolds as little more than a "bus driver," but Reynolds had done some hard time. He'd been with the military ever since he was eighteen down in Panama, where he'd once double-fisted a dancer named Mercedes while waiting to do his part in the overthrow of the country's military dictator, Manuel Noriega.

"That's where we're going," said Rami. "See the black stuff?"

I could just barely make out the heaped acres of smoking charcoal cooking in the distant sands to the west. Reynolds clipped pictures. Rami stood with his hands on the hips of his blue jeans. He was wearing a beige ball cap and a white T-shirt with a blue rhinoceros on the chest. We walked across the causeway, looked out at the Euphrates valley, the curve of the river marked by a tight green cluster of date palms on the left, the west bank. As we passed over the dam we looked down into the top of the occupied compound where a dozen or so marines in green shirts and desert cammies were cooking on barrel-drum barbecues. I could smell the meat and the smoke and feel the cool, moist air issuing from the reservoir and the river.

I felt hungry. I felt awake. But I did not feel scared of the air we were about to breathe. And why should I have been worrying about the burning garbage on the other side of the river? It wasn't on our side, the east side, and nobody was talking about burn pits back in 2008. It wasn't until 2009, eight years after the start of the war in Afghanistan, that the U.S. government finally issued regulations for burning waste in the Global War on Terror. Until that mandate, "we" had been endangering our troops with these unregulated bonfires of explosives, rubber, batteries, pesticides, tires, wiring, animals, and human body parts. The dangers became more obvious after Joseph Hickman, who was a former marine and Guantánamo Bay guard, "contacted one hundred and twelve service members and contractors who had served" in Iraq and discovered that, of these 112, "thirty-one now suffered from different forms of cancers and brain tumors." This is a story that's been breaking thanks to journalists like Hickman. But to talk about our soldiers is only the beginning of the story. The burn pit Rami led me to that morning was run by the private military contractor Kellogg Brown & Root, ubiquitously known in military circles as KBR. These burn pits are part of a current, massive public health crisis that still impacts the people of Iraq.

"Iraq is poisoned," Joseph Hickman argues in his 2016 book *The Burn Pits: The Poisoning of America's Soldiers*. Eight years earlier I stood with Reynolds and Rami above an uncovered vat of black syrupy waste less than a quarter mile from the waters of the Euphrates River. This water source sustains the cities of Barawanah, Haqlaniyah, and Haditha downstream. I looked down on this black bilge and I didn't understand. I looked out on two separate smoking heaps of ash and rubble, the burning waste more a pile than a pit, an increasingly undifferentiated mound of hissing cinders decaying under what appeared to be strung-together skeletons, the transformers issuing power from the dam to the people. There were no KBR personnel present that day to warn us, to tell us to step away from the smoke, the feathery swarms of ashes. Here was what American outsourcing looked like in Iraq. Here was America's national deregulation manifested as international action, inaction in action. We walked right up to the toxic plume beneath the shadow of the dam. Not far away, in the war-torn city of Fallujah, Al Jazeera reported that "the rate of local birth-defects was a shocking thirty-three times higher than in Europe." According to this same report, many of the people of Fallujah "have decided not to have children for fear of the shocking number of miscarriages, infant deaths and deformed or otherwise sick newborns. Many of the birth defects being seen in Iraqi hospitals are so rare that there is no medical term for them." These are the early reports on what may be one of the worst environmental catastrophes of our time, the story of the Iraq War as an ecological disaster.

"So this is the burn pit," Rami said.

Based on Rami's attire that day—the jeans and short-sleeved T-shirt with the rhino logo—I have to conclude that he was as unconcerned about the health effects as I was. Maybe, like me, he just believed he would never reach old age. In any event, there we were, standing in the middle of history like caricatures of American idiocy: we were the rubes, the ones snapping pictures and taking off our shirts near what should have been a Superfund site and might well constitute a war crime.

We wandered farther into the desert, found an abandoned and utterly rusty Iraqi tank that was so perforated with bullet holes from target practice that I was afraid it would crumble if I touched it. But I did more than touch it. Like a child at the state fair, I got on the old ride. I stood triumphantly on top of the tank and asked Reynolds to take a picture of me. I jumped down. I noticed so many bullet casings in the sand I felt like I was surrounded by fossilized maggots.

Yes, much as I wanted to forget it, there was no denying this was a war zone. According to the stats Reynolds had shared with me prior to my embed, there had been on average 144 attacks a day in Al Anbar Province—this region—as late as May 2006. By February 2008 they were down to 155 a month, but that was still 155 more than I wanted to encounter—or am I lying? Here was a region with 70 percent unemployment, constant kidnapping, regular beheadings on the soccer fields, an American massacre still in very recent memory, and now a toxic burn pit to boot, perhaps our generation's equivalent of the Agent Orange tragedy right under my nose, and what was I doing? I was practically skipping. I had never in my life felt so alive as I did over there on the edge of death. I was snorting war like it was some kind of amphetamine.

I took pictures. I stood right over the Haditha burn pit and ignored my rational voice, what may well have been my survival instinct or the voice of my father, the doctor. Instead, what I followed was something else: the hunger to see things for myself.

That night after witnessing the burn pits for the first time, I ambled over to the snack hut to watch some TV and fry up a cheeseburger. Inside I found Rami with two or three soldiers either waiting for their turn to play video games or just enjoying the camaraderie of watching others, just being in the room with people instead of isolating one's self in those Conex boxes and the shaky forms of refuge one might find online.

Rami and I didn't talk about the burn pits. And nobody greeted me the way they did Unis at the police station, but no one was unkind either. I didn't feel unwelcome, but I also did not have the sense that anyone was eager to tell a particular story or spill any particular can of beans. But maybe it was just as well. I was still early in my embed, still getting to know this unit of men. Maybe the wisest course of action was to just be in the moment and take notes. I opened up the freezer because Diet had told me to help myself while at the same time suggesting that I try not to be "Eat Boy."

"Fuck!" said the soldier who had just lost his turn in whatever video game he was playing.

I nuked a burger and opened up a Pepsi with a portrait of a beautiful Iraqi actress printed on the can, Arabic letters and the seductive face of this woman dislocating the standard experience of sipping on this red, white, and blue cylinder of soda. I want to remember those men embracing me convivially as I sat down with my burger and soda. I want to recall a dialogue in which I can unpack for you that meeting with the mayor and that visit to the school and the burn pits, the ticking-clock fear I felt on the open road as I wondered if death in the form of an IED was just around the bend. But I don't remember the men asking me a single question as I took a seat on the riser in front of the big-screen TV. What I remember is feeling what I constantly felt in Iraq, a kind of impostor syndrome, a pressure to perform the role of the journalist, to ask the questions that needed to be asked, to summon such questions out of the blue.

"What are y'all playing?" I asked.

I'd been introduced to a lot of guys already. Was I in the room with Scotty and Tree? Or was it B-Dubbs and Lurch? I know it wasn't Andrew, the kind, blond-haired soldier who would play his synthesizer for me one night and give me a pair of green, white, and black Iraqi soccer pants to take home as a memento. I can't reliably tell you who was in the room with me that night, but I do remember a large cache of DVDs in a box or a drawer near the screen and that there was talk of watching *Lions for Lambs* after the guy who was playing video games was done.

I remember finally getting into a conversation with someone and being so grateful for the company that I lied when he asked me who I worked for. Instead of telling this soldier that I was in Iraq working for a magazine named *Convergence Quarterly* and that we hadn't even published a single issue yet, I told him that I worked for my small hometown newspaper, the *Winchester Star*. I emphasized our proximity to DC and the fact that our editor was a Byrd, hoping such name-dropping would buy me credibility, but I also emphasized that we were a small-town newspaper, to assure this soldier that whatever he told me would likely not be seen by the eyes of the world.

"Small-town papers started Abu Ghraib," the guy said.

I went quiet after he said that. I'm pretty sure this was Scotty, Diet's second-in-command. I ate my burger and watched a real Navy SEAL tense up and curse and laugh as he simulated slaughter through his soldier avatar in *Halo 2*. I liked video games when I was a kid, particularly *Super Mario Bros.* and *One on One: Dr. J vs. Larry Bird*, but I never made the transition into the first-person POV shooter games. Just like I didn't feel equipped to talk about the dam or damn near anything, I wasn't quite sure how to open up a conversation about video games and what they meant or whether such a line of questioning was even worth pursuing.

I finally put in a dip to calm my anxiety and took some notes on what I'd seen so far. I kept coming back to Captain Al'a and his mullet and the kidnapping on Baje Road, the fact that people were disappearing all the time out here. I continued to document the folklore of the war, the graffiti I'd find in the latrines:

> *Hillary's a communist. She can't service her man. How can she*
> *serve a country?*
> *I fucked your mom with a baseball bat.*
> *Right now your mom's boyfriend is beating your kid.*
> *In death is redemption.*
> *Kill all fags.*

I spit wintergreen tobacco juice into the punctured top of the erotic Iraqi Pepsi can. The soldier in *Halo 2* was moving in rapid vectors through lunar wastes, a landscape of ruined columns and sandstone structures resembling the Iraqi cityscapes we'd visited that day. When I asked the guys waiting their turn to play to identify their biggest complaint about the war, one said, "We're not getting enough kills. We're trained to kill, but this is what we fucking do most days of the week." He pointed to the heads exploding on the screen.

Later that night, after watching *Lions for Lambs* with the guys (a decently didactic movie more notable for its cast than its plot), I asked Diet that same question. We were back in his Conex box, surrounded by the Christmas lights and the blankets from Pakistan, the pinup girls, and the photo of his father. He said, "I've been away from my family for three years, Eat Boy. I don't know how to need anybody anymore. I mean, what do I really need that I can't do myself?"

This strikes me now as a rather revealing complaint. I think it would be an understatement to say that many Americans value independence. I know I do. But Diet seemed to be second-guessing his military life in that moment, which is to say, his life. Through his tours of Iraq, the Philippines, and beyond, he had learned the tools of self-reliance: how to rely on a brother for warmth in the shivering cold of the Pacific Ocean during BUDS (Basic Underwater Demolition), how to survive in the tropical wilderness, how to masturbate one's self through pangs of desire and regret, how to kill another man if need be, how to erase the big picture of the state for the focal point of the platoon, and how to manage the day-to-day trauma of mortar attacks and imminent IEDs. With such powers of survival under one's belt, did one really need a nuclear family?

"How are your folks?" I asked, impersonating Diet's father who always, with military precision, asked exactly that question to start conversations with Diet's friends.

I could try to work Diet's voice like a ventriloquist's puppet here and mime the way I think he answered that question by briefly summarizing the lives of his older sister and brother and how they too were still single, but I didn't keep impeccable notes on my conversations with Diet because it felt like a sin to do so and it still feels like a sin to mention anything more than the general feeling of the time we spent in that room. My understanding was that what happened in that room was not classified but private, and by saying that, I do not mean to suggest any homosexual high jinks ensued between Diet and Eat Boy—between my friend and me. What I mean to say is that there are parts of this story that I feel need to be told and there are a million details that might qualify as clever, subversive, or perverted but have nothing to do with the story I want to tell. And part of that story involves people who think that their truth needs to be told in order to understand how America got in this mess we're still calling the war on terror. To me, it seems clear that we can't talk about that mess without talking about secrecy.

I do not believe we should all wear chips under our clavicles. I do not believe that every friend should second-guess his most intimate conversations with his or her best friends in the twenty-first century because a hidden mic or camera might be on for someone's followers-slash-customers on Twitter or Facebook or for the NSA. I do not believe that "telling the truth" about every personal detail that was disclosed in that Conex box in Iraq is essential to me telling you the story of what I discovered over there. I want to protect Diet, just as I know he wanted to protect me. He is my friend and nothing has strained our friendship more than my feeling of a need to talk about the things I discovered in Iraq. Diet may have lost the sense of need through war, but I obtained the opposite feeling. Diet may have found the ability to shut off the world through the classified tasks of his units, but the secret tasks of all of our units that my meager tax dollars blindly supported had left me feeling estranged from my own country. What I can tell you is this: our conversations—our time together in Iraq—forever altered our friendship and the ways in which we saw ourselves—and each other—in this world.

"Eat Boy in Iraq," he said over and over during our time together on the Euphrates.

Like he couldn't believe his opposite—his friend—had arrived. Like this was some great prank, which it kind of was: two boyhood friends having a slumber party in the middle of the war-torn desert. We surfed the net together, Skyped with our mutual friend, Cooter. We turned off the lights and, like the kids we once were, curled up in sleeping bags beneath a Ping-Pong table. We talked in the dark while listening to music on Diet's MacBook. The conversation roamed freely, as conversations between friends will. I talked about Karen and how I'd nearly gotten into a fight one night when she'd called me to come to her house—our old house—to protect her from some drunken suitor who was threatening to steal Evildoer, our—her—Jack Russell.

"This is what you get for dating a stripper," Diet said.

I laughed uncomfortably. But I also defended Karen, as if she were still mine. I told Diet that she was also a zookeeper and a human being.

"Who do you think will be the last of us to marry?" he asked.

"I'm betting on me," I said.

"I'm betting on me," he said.

We made a wager that night, the stakes of which I can't remember. We continued to talk about our lost loves and our old friends and how the powers that be were tearing down the orchards of our hometown of Winchester, Virginia. The Grateful Dead played low and the intricate designs of those Pakistani prayer rugs spoke of other lives in the dim darkness. I will never forget the breathless way we both laughed after a call and response series of farts and Diet, like a chorus, saying one more time, "Eat Boy in Iraq. Jesus fucking Christ. Eat Boy in Iraq."

The next day I met one of the Iraqis who lived downstream from the burn pits. His name was Sheikh D'han Hussein D'meithan Al Jughayfi. He had pouchy eyes and wore a brown silk robe with golden trim, a red-and-white *ghutra*, which looked to me like a tea cloth fastened to his head by a black band. He was about my father's height, roughly five foot nine, and his black mustache was flecked with gray. I was now with a new translator, Salah, a thin, middle-aged man. He sat to the sheikh's right while I sat in front of the sheikh and sipped one of those sexy Pepsis.

"I like the coalition," the sheikh told me after I started him with one of my broad Larry King–esque questions, something like, "What do you make of this war?"

Diet stood over us, and so did Reynolds. I held my marbled black-and-white lab notebook in my lap and wrote down the translated answers Salah gave me. The sheikh emphasized that he was not present that day for financial gain. He claimed he was not a Baathist. He said that he used to have money but that now he was poor and selling everything he owned. He didn't have a vehicle. He lived in his father's house and told me that Saddam Hussein's rule had been devastating for his people.

"The regime destroyed me," he said.

This was not the image of a sheikh that I had anticipated. Growing up in America, the only sheikh I knew was the professional wrestler known as the Iron Sheikh, a big, broad-chested man known for his bluster and strength, the fact that he had once been the bodyguard for the shah of Iran, the despot the United States inserted after overthrowing the first democratically elected leader in Iran's history, Mohammad Mossadegh. The Iron Sheikh suggested that sheikhs were near equals in strength and danger to American celebrity heroes like Hulk Hogan. The Iron Sheikh projected a haughty and ridiculous caricature of the Middle East. I never imagined someone could be a sheikh and be broke and illiterate, living in his father's house.

"It's all bullshit," Salah said to me at one point.

"Mutar saif," I said back, trying to impress this future CIA agent with the Arabic phrase for bullshit Moni had gifted to me in Kuwait. I turned a page in my journal, as if to search for my next set of questions. But there was no next set of questions. So I asked about the sheikh's family.

"Eighteen people in my family have been killed in the war," he said.

This comment would stand out in stark contrast to later in the conversation, when the sheikh would argue "there are no dangerous people in Haditha." There was definitely a recurrent pattern of bullshit in the comments I was receiving from Iraqis and Americans alike. Near the end of my interview, as if aware that I wasn't buying his story, the sheikh lifted his robe and pointed furiously at his hairy left leg, where I could see, just above the wasted elastic of his dark brown sock, a large, white, heart-shaped growth rimmed in black. This was not a birthmark.

"I have sons," the sheikh said. "One is Iraqi police. One repairs taxis. But I have no money anymore because of the cancer of my son. He has had thirty-nine operations. Bone-marrow transplants. Chemotherapy."

The sheikh again pointed at the growth on his left leg. I asked him what he thought to be the cause of the cancer. He looked worried. He said, "I want the coalition to stay. I'll pick up my whole family and go with them. I just want peace. Safety."

I believed that last part, and I believed what I photographed on the sheikh's leg. I was oblivious to so much when I was in Iraq, but I had a feeling that Rami had taken me to that riverside burn pit for a reason, that as a translator from a neighboring country he felt a deeper connection to this landscape than to his employers. I had no idea that the burn pits were an emergent international health crisis, but that day, sitting with the sheikh, I did have a sense that something not so mysterious was causing cancer downstream and bankrupting Iraqi families, sending them into a state of ruin and despair. Whistle-blower Chelsea Manning released classified documents from as early as December 20, 2006, establishing that the U.S. military was aware of "burn pit health hazards." Manning went to prison for the intelligence she shared, the story our country tried to keep secret. As far as I know, the photographs I took of the Haditha burn pit are the only ones in the public record. I wonder now, as I look back at the yellowing pages of my notes from that conversation with Sheikh D'han Hussein D'meithan, if he and his son are still alive, how many other Iraqis are out there with these strange symptoms, and what the burn pits have to do with such stories, if anything.

What we do know now is that American soldiers, with their brief exposures, are suffering from burn pit fallout to such a degree that a Republican congressional representative from North Carolina, Thom Tillis, has acknowledged this tragedy and sought government compensation for our troops together with Sen. Amy Klobuchar, a Democrat from Minnesota. But our troops are lucky. In spite of the Beau Bidens and the thousands of less famous veterans now suffering from respiratory infections, neurological disorders, deformed children, and cancer, these men and women were able to get away from the rivers and the winds of Iraq. What about the people who remain in that land of sandstorms, where air and land often seem one? What if you were the sheikh's son and you survived your own cancer after your thirty-nine operations? What if, best-case scenario, the sheikh himself, despite bankruptcy, survived alongside his son? If you were an old man or a young man living in Haditha after

American forces left, what would you make of the scarred land upstream from your village, the ashen remains of occupation? And, perhaps more unsettling, what would you make of the occupying forces the Arab media called DAESH, the ones the American media called ISIS? What would you think of these soldiers with their messages of purification and unification, their hatred of America? If you were the son of the sheikh, with cancer in your bloodstream and the choice was between conceiving a child with that corrupted blood or leaving domesticity behind and joining the dystopian rebel forces upstream, where would you throw your lot? When I put my arm around the sheikh at the end of our interview, I smiled for the camera. The sheikh did not.

# 6. NOVEMBER 2007

## AMERICA

Fighting for peace is like fucking
for virginity.

—GRAFFITI FROM THE WAR

I tasted death for the first time when I was four at a place my family called
The Lake, as if there were no other lake in the world. We Armstrongs
were lake people, descended from the roisterous clans that roamed about
the lochs and tarns of Scotland. My father grew up on Strawberry Lake,
just outside of Detroit. Later the family moved a few miles away, to Gilbert Lake. After moving us from Michigan to Virginia, my father began
to look for a lake of his own, and he found one, a place called Lake Holiday. For Christmas in 1981 he bought us a new red canoe. On a twenty-
degree day in January 1982 something propelled my father out of the
house, past the old Shawnee village at the cross-junction, and up Route
522 toward West Virginia. The Lake can be found a few miles south of
the West Virginia state line.

Even though The Lake was frozen, the boys of the family had a job
to do: deliver the new red canoe to The Lake. Frost powdered the dead
vegetation as we drove past the half-developed land around The Lake in
our gray Oldsmobile station wagon with colorful arcade upholstery in the
back. We parked in the gravel lot down by the marina. My older brother,
Andy, must have been the one to help my father remove the canoe from

the roof of the Olds, or maybe my father did all the work himself while we sprinted down the pier, amazed by the crystal surface of The Lake.

Andy was eight that day at The Lake. Back home, my mother nursed our new baby sister, Katee. Maybe that was the reason we were up at The Lake: somebody needed space. Maybe my father drove to The Lake that day for the reason I now go to the lakes of Greensboro: just to feel the stillness of that landscape, so different from a river.

From the marina my brother and I faced what we called "the B side," the undeveloped forest pileated with pines, hemlock, and spruce, hints of the Michigan woods, the whisper of the wilderness past on the winter wind of the present. My brother and I sat at the end of the pier with our feet dangling over the ice, Matchbox cars in the pockets of our winter coats. We looked down at the surface of The Lake with the eyes of boys. We took out our Matchbox cars: a black Firebird and a red, white, and blue Captain America.

We lay down on our bellies. Andy guided his Firebird in tight, furious circles, making the sounds of an engine, lines in the frost. I did the same. I imitated my brother. When Andy let his Firebird slide across the slick surface, I did the same, but my Captain America went too far. I couldn't reach it with my short arms, and rather than call for my father or ask for help from my big brother, I ran out onto the ice.

The ice held until the ice broke. The water filled my pockets. I rose up, only to hit my head against the bottom of the top, triggering years of dreams: suffocations, cul-de-sacs, apneal moments I've never fully shaken out of the recesses of my mind. I see only the bolts of gold when I remember those seconds, a frozen flash of dark water shot through with wild light, the thick sheet of ice rejecting my surge. I hit my head on the ice and went under, but my brother reached down and found my hand. Andy saved my life. A reductive but not entirely unproductive way of looking at our relationship emerged from that moment: death-teaser and lifesaver, prodigal and loyal. He was the doctor. I was the guy in a rock band called Viva la Muerte.

When I was eighteen and my brother was twenty-one, we were once mistaken for twins. We both had our father's blue eyes, that same Scottish tendency to go extremely red in the face during moments of anger and exertion, competition. When we were younger we both wore our brown hair in that acceptably wingy way that was popular among white privileged soccer players in the Virginia suburbs of the nineties, just as it was also trendy to occasionally reveal the bottoms of your boxers below your shiny soccer shorts. I learned that look from Andy. When he worshipped mock turtlenecks, I worshipped mock turtlenecks. When he bought braided belts, I bought braided belts. But then at some point I took off in my own direction, across the ice. I scrapped the turtlenecks, started wearing tie-dye. My brother studied medicine. I studied history. I dove down every rabbit-hole story I could find until I found the soldiers who got secret sicknesses nobody talked about. And so I began to return to my brother with questions about war.

Soon after my halfhearted attempt at reconciliation with Karen, Andy came to Greensboro to take me out for dinner at a now defunct rooftop restaurant on the north side of Elm Street. There was now no mistaking who was who. I was the shaved head with the goatee, the one who spent too much time working on his biceps. Andy was the one who allowed his hair to recede for all to see, who adopted no cover for the soft family chin. Andy didn't obsess with vanity, or at least did not seem to. Andy appeared to accept himself, the changes of age and circumstance gracefully incorporated, embraced. Andy spoke softly, but forcefully.

"Karen called us," he said. "She's worried about you."

At first I thought this was a good sign. Yes! My emotionally abusive allusion to suicide had worked and Karen now cared again! Yes!

"What's she worried about?" I asked.

I had said so much in the Gold's Gym parking lot that I honestly didn't think about any one utterance having gained particular purchase in my ex.

"She said you guys talked the other day," Andy said. "She said you're threatening to hurt yourself. Is that true?"

At first I was stunned by the irony, the dark mirror. Karen had once cut herself to convince me to stay after I'd attempted to break up with her. It worked. I stayed. But I never thought *I* was that kind of person until that night. I was the mature and fearless one, right?

"Andy, Karen's crazy," I said.

"You didn't tell her you wanted to kill yourself?"

"No."

"She said you did."

"I told her I was thinking of going to Iraq, Andy. I think she's just flipping out about it, like Dad. Did I tell you he called Diet's dad to try to convince him to convince Diet to convince me not to go? I'm trying to be a writer and I get the assignment of my life, and this is what he does. He's trying to sabotage me."

"He just cares about you. This has been a rough year for him. Think about it. We all care about you. We love you."

It was hard to stay hard and defiant in the face of those words. It had been an extremely rough year for my father. His father's leukemia had come back, and he—my grandfather, whom I called Bumpa—was finally ready to call it quits, to stop the blood transfusions. Bumpa was ready to die. My father's cousin, Richie, had just died of an aneurysm. My mother's cancer had recently entered a remission, but it still haunted us all with the possibility of return. For a brief moment, sitting on that rooftop with Andy, watching anonymous pedestrians walk under the arc lights of Elm Street, my brother's empathetic words gave me a sense of what it was like to be walking in my father's shoes.

"But what about them?"

Yeah. What about them, Matt, the ones right across from you. Your father. Your brother. Dear god, I could feel it as I looked into Andy's eyes. My brother was afraid because my father was afraid. My family was afraid. Karen was afraid. My father was feeling vulnerable, like his life was under attack and I was blind to that. My father—my hero—wanted to keep the people he loved alive and together, and he was afraid he was about to lose that battle, his entire family. The love of the people all around me was not entirely lost on me. I knew my family loved me, but I also knew that their love was sliding into fear, and without any evidence on my side except for the circumstantial—the call from Diet—I began to yield to that fear, and instead of yielding to vulnerability I took the other path and became convinced that my father was the reason the *Winchester Star* had revoked my sponsorship. Did I yield to my brother that night? No. Did I believe in a paternal conspiracy to keep me from being the writer I wanted to be? Yes, I did.

I listened to my brother at dinner that night, but driving back to Colfax, I dug out an old tape, my favorite album from when I was fifteen: *Rage against the Machine*. The song I listened to was "Killing in the Name," that great angry antifascist howl, Zack de la Rocha and I screaming together at the end of the song, telling some white supremacist control freak authority figure to fuck himself over and over and over again.

In that moment the people who loved me were nothing more than the forces of evil trying to keep me from seeing the racist war they supported, and there was no way in hell I was going to let them convince me that my desire to see the truth of the war was really just some fearful charade, a fool's way of concealing his pain.

"Fuck you!" I screamed at the night.

I paced "the cabin." I dialed the first few digits of Karen's number. I took a walk outside under the November trees. I just couldn't shake my hunch that someone was fucking with my life, and I felt like I knew who it was. It was the same guy who was calling Diet's dad, treating me like I was still fifteen. I called home and talked to my mother, demanding to know if my father had called Tom Byrd.

"I'm not getting into this," she said.

"Mom," I said. "Tell me."

"I am not saying a word," she said.

That was all I needed to hear. My mother was my best friend, and we'd always had a deal when it came to the truth: if I told it, no matter what I'd done, I wouldn't get in trouble. This arrangement largely pertained to the ingestion of psychedelic drugs during my last two years of high school, but it carried over and led to the two of us having an unusually open conversation about life from that point on. I would tell her the strange truths of my life, and she would return the favor. The way she evaded my question about my father's meddling—the way she kept saying, "I'm not getting into this"—every time I pressed the issue, was the best she could do to avoid taking sides, to stay loyal to both me and my father. It was like Diet and his rhetoric of "cleaning up the mess." I knew right then with that single coded phrase—"I'm not getting into this"—that I was on to something.

Conventional wisdom always seems to suggest that the frantic, paranoid mind, be it the man's or the woman's, needs to be disabused of its "hysterical" notions, its intuitions, its hunches about conspiracy and plot, secret interventions. I have touted that conventional masculine wisdom, that "chill out, bitch be cool" caution. I have tried to coax many students down from their mountaintops of apocalyptic fear, their declarations of belief in secret, privileged societies and cabalistic coups, inside jobs, conspiracies. I have tried to take the middle ground, brokering a peace between the extremists and the cynics in my classrooms (and mind), acknowledging that conspiracies exist from time to time (see Caesar and Watergate) but that we must still employ critical thinking. But the moment my mother told me "I'm not getting into this," I knew with a zealot's fervor that my father was the Wizard of Oz and I was getting played like a puppet. It was at that point the world seemed more dangerously clear than it ever had before.

After I got off the phone with my mother I took a long walk past the dark horse farm to my right and past the house of a neighbor who'd recently allowed an old unemployed friend to park his rusty Winnebago in his front yard. I felt the confusion of the dogs I heard in the distance. I needed to learn how to stay . . . stay . . . stay. I felt the beached despair of the orange light in that stranger's rusty Winnebago, a life that had perhaps gotten out of hand or was just now burning out. I looked up at the stars and felt the same burning aspiration I'd known for years, felt blessed to still know that feeling, to not have to psychologize it away as mania or delusion or entitlement or bipolar disorder. The flame I felt in my mind was a righteous anger and its target was not some hard-to-prove secret society of bankers and politicians. It was my father.

"Eat Boy, you're a man," Diet had said.

But my father seemed to disagree. I didn't yet know exactly what he'd done, but I knew that this battle we were in was my crucible, my test, my chance to prove that I was a man. My father wanted to eat his cake and have it, too. He wanted to argue with me that George W. Bush's war was right and that it was good for us to be in Iraq, to be going to what Dick Cheney called the "dark side." But my father didn't want his son to see that dark side, that war, that good thing. And why not? I wanted to see the thing for myself. I wanted to be a man. I wanted to see it, this mess we were making, these lives we were saving. I didn't want to kill anyone, but I wanted to be part of "we" and this chaos, this awakening, whatever it was. I wanted to see our war. I wanted to see what rich men voted for and then ignored. I wanted to know what it was like to live the other kind of life, the one Diet was living, the life of service and blind faith where you took your orders and your father was proud and the source of life was the risk of death.

Thanksgiving was fast approaching, all the leaves falling from the trees, the geese flying in Vs, the teachers bitching, the students slacking, the news dividing up the world between the Left and the Right. I didn't want to go home to my father defeated or angry, but I didn't know what to do about sponsorship. In order to enter the desert of the real, the ostensibly unmediated realm of war, I needed to get my media situation together. During office hours one day I stopped by the wobbly gray cubicle of Kevin Rippin, a wonderful, curmudgeonly man, a penguin-shaped poet from Johnstown, Pennsylvania.

"Matty," Rippin crowed out of the corner of his mouth like some Brooklyn wiseguy. Rippin was busy at work on a book of narrative poems about his neighborhood, a series of surreal vignettes about suburban America. Most of these poems seemed inspired by his wife, a woman who'd once been a student of his at Greensboro College, where we'd both worked before A&T. She now had a law degree but didn't work. She often slept until three or four in the afternoon.

"How's your wife's new job?" I'd always say.

"What new job?" Rippin would bark.

Then we'd laugh, and sometimes he'd share one of his poems and then we'd talk about it, and sometimes I'd think, *This man understands the art of life*. He doesn't get caught up in war and history, things he can't control. He doesn't run away from his relationship, in spite of his burden. He works diligently on his chapbooks of parodic poetry. He makes people laugh. He supports his wife. He overcomes.

"Still going to Iraq?" Rippin asked.

"I don't know," I said. "The newspaper withdrew their sponsorship. I'm kinda screwed."

"What the fuck happened?"

I wanted to tell Rippin everything, but I hadn't yet talked to my father and I didn't want to scare Rippin with my anger, my theories. After all, he was a colleague. I didn't want to appear unstable.

"They claimed I don't have any experience in a war zone," I said.

"Didn't they know that in the fucking beginning?"

"I guess they talked to their lawyers," I said.

Rippin shook his head, motioned me outside so he could smoke a cigarette. We threaded our way through the grid of cubicles, bored students waiting for their instructors on orange plastic chairs outside the office, the drinking fountain in that building always delivering a suspiciously silty variety of water, those moments of smoke outside a Sisyphean respite from the lassitude and the halogen and the technological imperatives that substituted for a coherent curricular vision.

"I gotta get the fuck out of this place," Rippin said.

"That's what I was trying to do," I said.

Rippin offered me a cigarette. For the first time in a while, I took one. It tasted good. We talked. I cherished these moments. After breaking up with Karen and moving to the country, I found myself craving human interaction in a way that I never had before. I was lonely. I did everything I could to fill up the void that love had left. Rippin told me the story of how in the early 1980s, while working for a small magazine, he'd traveled to Israel.

"It was right after that bombing in Beirut," Rippin said. "You remember that?"

"Nineteen eighty-three, right?"

Giving the accurate date was my way of avoiding the question. I was only six in 1983, so I didn't remember Beirut, but I did know about it and didn't want to seem too young to relate. I wanted Rippin to keep talking.

"It was just a little magazine," he said. "But it was good pay, and I'll never forget it. Different world over there. Fucking Reagan. Not good, Matty. I will tell you that. Not fucking good."

Rippin blew smoke into the sky. Maybe I exhaled through my nose the way I sometimes do around seasoned smokers, trying to prove that I'm not the poser I am. My idea didn't come to me all at once that day, but a seed had just been planted: a little magazine. Yes, an itsy bitsy teeny-weeny little academic magazine.

"I need to find somebody else," was what I said to Rippin. "Any kind of publication. I just need somebody—some publication—to sign on the dotted line."

"If there's anything I can do to help, let me know," Rippin said.

They say a happy childhood is a curse upon a writer. If that's true, I'm doomed. I grew up with two parents who didn't dote on me but were always there when I needed them. My father loved my mother and my father loved us—his children. I know this because he showed it. Despite working eighty-hour weeks as an infectious disease specialist, he coached my soccer team nearly every season for seven years. He used to always read stories to me and my brother and sister in this old black-and-white houndstooth chair that sat under a brass rubbing of a saint's grave he'd made while traveling with my mother in Europe when they were newly-weds. Sometimes, in that chair, my father would read to us out of Lao-tzu for several minutes before embarking upon an improvised adventure story of his own. Whenever we'd stop paying attention, my father, instead of reprimanding us, would tickle us or put us in the "mix-master," a churning combine of fingers and legs and squeals of laughter and delight.

But things weren't perfect in our family. There were tensions, particu-larly after the election of George W. Bush. In spite of his interest in Taoism, my father was a Christian. He believed in an old-school Christian code of conduct: sacrifice and charity, fidelity to one's wife. So he despised Bill Clinton, thought him a moral midget, a terrible role model. One thing my father grasped—an opinion he and I both shared—is that young men are deeply influenced by the behavior of their leaders. When leaders cheat, cheating is tacitly condoned. When leaders lie, lying seems the path of victory. When George W. Bush arrived in office, I think my father believed, with his native midwestern Michigander optimism, that America was about to return to its rightful role as a beacon of probity and rectitude, the late-nineties dose of decadence and moral relativism exchanged for a vintage bouquet of wartime righteousness and religious purification.

After 9/11 and a brief period of humility, my father and I took widely divergent paths. In 2003, on a family outing to Harpers Ferry, we had an extremely heated public argument at a barbecue joint. Was the root of it all my belief that there was no cause for invading Iraq? Was it my father comparing George W. Bush to Abraham Lincoln? Was it me bringing up the incendiary example of John Brown, a white American willing to attack his own country in order to save his own country?

"Enough!" my mother screamed that day—a rare moment of shrill intervention. My mother used to love our debates. But the flavor had changed from sweet to sour. The divide between my father and me on George W. Bush and his Global War on Terror may seem like a fairly typical conservative/liberal split, but the growing tension between this father and this son post 9/11 was not that of a liberal versus a conservative. I was and still am appalled by the flaccid catering of the Left. I was and still am attracted to the idea of a less intrusive government, particularly when it comes to sex and the military. I don't like our country telling its citizens who they can love, and I don't like our country having bases and wars all over the world. But what I cannot stand, and what I find to be evil, is the exploitation of religion and spirituality for the purposes of profit and political gain, using god to sell death to the poor. To say this is not to say that I believed my father condoned selling death to the poor in the form of the Iraq War. I may be biased, but I consider my father to be a wise and good man. One of my reasons for believing in him is his humility. Shortly before Thanksgiving my father called me to apologize for lying to me, a confession that nearly broke my heart before I subsequently thereafter offered him a lie of my own.

"It's okay, Dad," I said. "It's not a big deal. I found another magazine willing to sponsor me."

"Who?"

"You think I'm going to tell you after what you just told me?"

"Fair enough," he said.

My father laughed uneasily. What he had just admitted was that he had in fact spoken to his patient, Tom Byrd, and reminded Byrd, diplomatically, that a newspaper was legally responsible for its writers. Later my truth-telling mother elaborated and told me that my father had made his comments to Byrd during a checkup, a visit to my father's office for a trip that he, Byrd, was about to take with his wife. I don't know if my father used the term "potential lawsuit" or "liability," and I don't know if he stated his reservations about my embed while Tom Byrd was clothed or naked or perhaps wearing a paper gown. Was there a stethoscope on Byrd's heart as my father discussed my safety and welfare, or a needle in a vein, a hammer on a knee? Were his nuts clutched? What would you have done if you were in the editor's shoes and your newspaper was hemorrhaging cash as the internet took over the country? Do you side with the inexperienced son, the broke writer? Or do you listen to the insinuations of your doctor, your peer, your friend, a man like you, with lawyers at his disposal?

These days there's a lot of talk in this country about wealth, the 1 percent versus the 99. As an individual, I know I belong to the latter, not the former. I've been evicted. I've been on unemployment. I've worked fast food. I've worked construction. I've attended community dinners and sat side by side with the homeless dining on bruised vegetables and stale breads extracted by dumpster divers from the garbage of corporate supermarkets. Be this as it may, I've always known, if worse came to worst, that I live my life above a net, and even though I, as an individual, live in the 99, my family sits firmly in the 1.

"But what about them?" my father asked me before I left for Iraq.

But what about the "them" here at home, the poor who get sold on bullshit wars as a way out of the gutter, generation after generation? For most of my adult life I have lived with one foot in the 1 percent and the other in the 99. A few years before I traveled to Haditha, that city of 70 percent unemployment, I met a woman who opened my eyes. In 2004 I traveled with my then girlfriend, Karen, to the city that supplied Haditha with a good portion of its invaders. The day after George W. Bush defeated John Kerry, Karen and I, in the first year of our relationship, drove to Fayetteville together for the first time. Otherwise known as "Fayette-nam," Fayetteville, North Carolina, was Karen's hometown, a broken-down, sprawled-out military city whose life was organized around war and Fort

Bragg, the massive army post spread out on our right as we drove toward her mother's house. Among the fast food restaurants and shut-up store-fronts were more strip clubs than I'd ever seen before in my life. When I inquired about the plethora of purple neon, Karen said,

"Fucking military lifestyle."

Simple as that.

My family's 1 percent money had taken me all over the Western world—England, France, Switzerland, Germany, Jamaica, Mexico, the Caribbean, Canada—but as of that day in 2004 I'd really seen nothing of American poverty, that military-industrial brand of waste and despair that manifests itself in burned-out neon marquees, amputees in wobbly wheelchairs doing doughnuts in a weedy vacant lot, women like my new girlfriend, riddled with anxiety, covered in half-finished tattoos, driven by a desire to escape the carnality of this kind of life while at the same willing to use her knowledge of that life to make her escape.

Karen was working at a club in Greensboro when we first met. This was a secret we were both trying to keep from our parents. My mother and I may have had a deal about the truth, but it was my job to not extend the privileges of that deal to Karen's mother. We parked in a small drive-way in front of a small home in a neighborhood of other small homes.

"Please please please don't bring up politics," Karen said.

It was a gray, overcast night, the mood infused with a postelection gloom (for us), the sad, droopy patrician face of John Kerry in his conces-sion speech flitting constantly in my mind. How had this veteran with real wartime credentials lost to a man like Bush?

"What happened to your voice? Fight!" I wanted to tell Kerry. "Chal-lenge the results in Ohio, you goddamn pussy!"

Kathy, Karen's mother, greeted us at the door with a warm hug. Kathy had a kind but tired face, short, shoulder-length orange hair atop a sturdy Polish physique that, I soon learned, was capable of doing all the work around the house. Kathy showed us around, pointed out the busted wall of a bedroom undergoing renovation. In the backyard she introduced me to a frazzle-haired, popcorn-colored mutt whose crazy fur suggested that perhaps it had just taken a toke from an electrical socket.

I looked for signs of the cult Karen had grown up in, the Worldwide Church of God. I wondered if I would see the last name of their charismatic leader—Armstrong—on the spines of the books on Kathy's shelf. This is probably not the place for talking about the controlling Old Testament spirit of Herbert Armstrong, but the synchronicity of our last names was always an unsettling private joke between Karen and me, a mystery we never fully explored.

I continued to look around her mother's house. I saw Christian literature among the high school photographs in the cramped living room. While we relaxed on a couch and talked about Karen and her love of animals and how she'd adopted an extremely large number of mice as a young girl—much to Kathy's chagrin—Karen bashfully retreated. She parked herself in front of an antique, slightly-out-of-tune piano and began to play. It goes without saying that my memory isn't perfect, but I believe the song she chose was Chopin's "Prelude in E Minor."

Kathy and I stopped talking. That house suddenly seemed bigger, like a cathedral, the Christian literature on the bookshelf suddenly a window into a searching soul rather than evidence of fundamentalist mind control. I watched Karen's fingers on the keys, the sudden softness in her eyes, the hint of a younger woman in her mother's features. Listening to the graceful but funereal sadness of that song, I remember thinking, *Jesus, this is it. I'm in love.*

Two years later and it was all over. Two years later, on Christmas Eve day, we were in my parents' home, arguing in my old bed under my old poster of John F. Kennedy, my attention divided between Karen's angry, accusatory face and the sound of my sick mother organizing silverware in the kitchen, that tinkling sound slowly giving way to sizzling and recorded classical music and the smell of French toast and bacon.

Throughout her life Karen had been abandoned by men, and to say "abandoned" does not just mean "left." These men—fathers, stepfathers, boyfriends—they did more than just leave her. They left the country. They hit her over the head with cans of soup. They kicked her in the stomach when she was pregnant. They slept with her friends. They drove her to the top of a mountain with a shovel in the trunk and told her to dig a hole for her own grave. They left her alone with her mother in Fayetteville, beached among the soldiers and strippers and abandoned animals that she'd adopted because she knew some simple ways to keep them—the animals—from running away.

Human beings were another story. As of that Christmas Eve morning, I was just another guy who could afford to leave, another dude who didn't know how to hang in there, another man about to ditch in spite of sophisticated self-conscious conversations we'd had about how her deepest fear was somebody leaving her because of her fear of somebody leaving her and the way it made her ideally suited to do the sort of anxious, graspy, envious, desperate things that make men leave women—like cutting one's self, putting a fist through a window, tossing plates across a kitchen, or, say, arguing endlessly about a flirtatious encounter at a bar from a year earlier while a man's mother is down in the kitchen with stage-four ovarian cancer possibly cooking one of the last holiday meals of her life.

Did you notice the way I just veered into the third person? Now, I know having just completed that sentence that I'm loading a good-sized heap of heroic self-pity and protection upon my narrative self. So allow me to add this: if I am constructing myself on these pages as some kind of usefully naive truth-teller attempting to speak of the walls that divide us from each other both at home and abroad, that's because that's the character I want to be, the higher self I strive for every day. But quite often that's not who I am. The truth is, sometimes I am a mess. I have huge issues with anger and fear. The year that all of this happened I felt like I was coming apart. I had grown terrified of love. I put a ring on Karen's finger and then broke up with her more than thirty times. I didn't feel I could handle her trauma, the pain—the entirety—of this woman who had rather courageously emerged out of a cult and a period of homelessness and countless abusive relationships. So I was constantly looking for an escape. That Christmas Eve morning, I was quite justifiably getting dressed down for driving Karen to the home of a woman whom I'd professed love to in a bar the year before (I love everyone when I'm drunk), our goal at that home being the delivery of some Christmas cake, but the gist of the visit, to Karen was, *You have no regard for my feelings, Matt Armstrong. You, Matt Armstrong, are oblivious to what it feels like to stand next to you in a doorway while this competitor of mine hugs you and accepts a*

*holiday loaf from you and your family, a family that is privileged like her*
*family and nothing like mine, and that means something and you should*
*know that, so quit pretending like you're some golden boy who doesn't get*
*what it's like to be me.*

"Do you ever think about what I feel?" was one of the things Karen
half whispered and half screamed that morning, a variation on my father's
question: "But what about them?"

I listened to my family downstairs, laughing among the sizzling and
clinking sounds. At that moment I wanted nothing more than to be
free of Karen's anger and anxiety, the pain and vulnerability I'd fallen in
love with two years earlier, the notes of Chopin no preparation for the
sleepless nights and soured mornings we'd come to know, the vicarious
shiverings and twitchings of our dogs, the shards of old family plates, the
evictions, the rise in blood pressure, the broken windows, the hunger for
pharmaceutical hiatus and pornographic refuge, the thoughts of suicide,
the growing belief that the road to marriage was much more a torturous
boot camp than a flower-petaled path of bliss.

"We're done!" I screamed. "Get the fuck out!"

I sent Karen down the road crying and alone on Christmas Eve day. I
retreated like a jelly-soaked fetus back into the womb of white privilege
for a few more hours, a meal of French toast, the blankets of my bed.
Karen called my friends from the highway, begging them to call me. I still
didn't have a cell phone (because I thought they were harbingers of evil),
and she was too embarrassed to call my parents, so I was able to remain
insulated from her voice. After staring at the poster of John F. Kennedy
over my bed for more than an hour, I walked outside to the driveway,
where my brother, my father, and my uncle Carl were shooting hoops.
Uncle Carl was the first to greet me, slapping a big meaty paw down on
my shoulder before saying, "You did the right thing."

In spite of the guilt I still feel over the way I handled things, I suspect
Carl was right. Regardless of blame, it was clear: I wasn't yet ready for
marriage, putting somebody else in front of myself. And I wasn't ready
to talk about it either. I didn't stay in the driveway to shoot hoops and
unpack the breakup. I kept walking down the street where I grew up,
Launchris Drive, until it turned into Jones Road. I turned left on Jones

Road and walked along the barbed-wire fence that ran parallel to an over-grown lot that was once a soccer field. I felt full of the dead open space all around me, the run of Stonebrook Creek, the distant black dots of cat-tle on the hillside of old man Rudolph's farm, the old Civil War wall that now divided the super rich from the kinda rich, the sharp, tight-bellied winter clouds overhead like a fleet of ghostly ships arriving safely in the harbor, a wedding that would never be. Then, on the road, I saw a station wagon approaching from the other direction. It came to a quick stop a few feet past me and then yawned into reverse. The window slid down.

"Matt?"

It was Samantha Borg, the high school homecoming queen I'd taken to the hoco dance twelve years earlier. She had a kid strapped in a car seat in the back, the shotgun empty.

"I just called off my engagement," I said without any kind of preface.

"Get in," she said.

I felt like I was in a dream, a time machine. After Samantha had flipped her vw Bug into Stonebrook Creek our junior year, I'd taken to giving her rides to school. We used to tell each other everything. To take those same roads that morning—the S turn, Cedar Creek Grade, Merriman's Lane—it felt like I was about to come full circle, like by ending things with Karen I was finally beginning something with my old best friend, Samantha. I could almost hear the sentimental cinematic soundtrack cranking up. I told her everything, just like old times. She listened kindly and patiently, just like old times. She dropped me off at the exact same spot she'd picked me up, telling me to take care.

"I gotta get back to Peter," she said.

Her husband, Peter, it turned out, had just come home from the war.

1. Captain Al'a. Nickel Base, Haditha, Iraq, 2008.

2. Captain Al'a, Rami, and the author. Nickel Base, Haditha, Iraq, 2008.

3. The Haditha dam. Nickel Base, Haditha, Iraq, 2008.

4. Ruins of an Iraqi tank. The Al Jazira desert, Haditha, Iraq, 2008.

5. KBR burn pit. Nickel Base, Haditha, Iraq, 2008.

6. KBR camp. Nickel Base, Haditha, Iraq, 2008.

7. Sheikh D'han Hussein D'meithan and the author. Nickel Base, Haditha, Iraq, 2008.

8. Stuck in a wadi of the Al Jazira desert. Haditha, Iraq, 2008.

9. Lucy in the garden. Nickel Base, Haditha, Iraq, 2008.

10. Self-portrait while leaving Haditha. Skies over Haditha, Iraq, 2008.

# 7. MARCH 2008

IRAQ

---

There are no weapons of mass
destruction in Iraq.
Chuck Norris lives in Oklahoma.
—GRAFFITI FROM THE WAR

I felt the clock ticking on my time in Haditha. I wanted to know more
about the destruction of the girls' school and the burn pits and the mysterious cancer downstream. I also wanted to meet with Captain Al'a one
more time and meet his Iraqi SWAT (ISWAT) team. Even if I wasn't a fan
of his cologne, I liked the captain and his candor, his seeming fearlessness
in the face of death. But the idea of a SEAL-trained independent strike
force with a brash, mulleted leader struck me as a risky proposition. To
me this sounded like a recipe for either rapid problem solving or imminent disaster. Maybe both. Diet scheduled another interview.

"But you should see this before we go," he said.

Seated in the dim light of his Conex box bedroom, he wheeled around
in his desk chair and motioned for me to watch a video on his laptop.

"Dear god, what is going on?" I asked, as I noticed a broken circle of
young Iraqis engaging in what at first seemed to be some kind of performance art. Some of the young camouflaged men were frozen in lunges
and squats and teapots. Others were jumping and scissoring in a disso-
nant array of calisthenics while an American drill instructor counted
out the routine.

"One! Two! Three!"

It was a video from about a month earlier, the sort of footage the American media would be perplexed with if asked to frame it for the public. Here were young Iraqi soldiers trying to become just like us. They were wearing our clothes and wielding our weapons and drilling our drills. Here were the most highly trained Hadithan soldiers attempting, I repeat *attempting*, to do nothing more than jumping jacks for their SEAL mentors, and it wasn't working. We're not talking about five-minute miles or high-stepping through tires or shredding dog targets here. We're talking jumping jacks, twenty guys looking like they've been pranked with itching powder, twenty guys looking like a boot camp for mimes and stooges, like they're frisking themselves for change, one of the young men holding the peak of his jumping jack for a good solid ten seconds at one point, the Cajun voice of the drill leader audible on the video: "Holy shit, maggot, are you fucking kidding me?"

Diet took a deep breath.

"I can't believe we're about to hand over the country," he said. "It's going to be *Planet of the Apes*."

Night had fallen outside Diet's room. We walked the planks that connected the bunkhouses of the men and emerged under the March stars to the sound of the Euphrates, the cool river smell of the night, the sounds of voices from down the way at the video game hut. A stray mongrel dog roamed across the grounds sniffing at the HESCO gabions.

"You getting some ideas?" Diet asked as we walked past the porta-johns and the sandbags and the concrete barricades lined up along the edge of the river. We climbed the steps toward the top of the dam, where, to the left, we were scheduled to meet with the SWAT team.

"I'm starting to get a vision for a novel," I said. "It's going to be called *Diet's Will*."

"So I'm going to die?" he said. "You're going to kill off your best character?"

I laughed at that.

He was right. He was my best character, and the novel I imagined during that time did indeed involve Diet getting burned alive and all his best boyhood friends gathering for his funeral and the reading of his will and then traveling to Iraq to find his killers like some kind of self-appointed civilian independent strike force, a SWAT team of thick white bros. Imagine the Iraqis who couldn't do jumping jacks and add fifty pounds and a hangover to each of them and you've got the idea. I don't want to say another word about it. The book was a disaster.

We took a moment at the top of the dam to have a dip and look down on the Euphrates. Fifteen years earlier Diet and I had both been freshmen at James Wood High School and taking World Cultures with Ms. Quesenberry, a teacher who would occasionally spice up her lessons about ancient civilizations with pictures of her in a bikini on spring break with the geometry teacher, Ms. Cregan. Now, here we were looking down on Mesopotamia, the land of ziggurats and Nebuchadnezzar and the Hanging Gardens, the Fertile Crescent where, before there was a Prophet Muhammad or a Jesus or a Yahweh, there were other, forgotten deities, like Marduk and Apsu and Tiamat. Apsu was the penile divinity, embodied by the Euphrates, who gave his teeming riparian load to the goddess of the sea: Tiamat.

We spit tobacco juice into the sacred sands and looked out on the stars and the distant lights of Haditha and Barawanah and Haqlaniyah. When we finally arrived at the ISWAT compound, I found Reynolds, Rami, and a number of Diet's men hanging out with the Iraqis as a soccer game played on a small TV. And there was Captain Al'a with his mullet and his same suit and same tie and shoulder holster, sitting behind a big desk at the rear of the room, a small vase of fake pink flowers to his right, a walkie-talkie with a rubber antenna to his left.

"Assalamu alaikum," I said to the captain.

The captain shook my hand over the desk and smiled. I could smell the Axe.

"Salaam," he said.

"Shlou-nek?" I asked, Arabic for "How are you?" Even though I'd memorized a few stock crib sheet questions like that, no way could I keep up with his long-winded response, which basically translated to an inventory of things (including electrical upgrades and boots) that his men needed.

Diet communicated through Rami that the captain's requests were being taken into consideration. Diet wore a hooded white Patagonia sweatshirt and desert camouflage pants that night. I wore a dark brown corduroy shirt. I took a seat in front of the desk as Diet and several of his men sat behind us in front of small tea tables. A member of the SWAT team who couldn't have been more than sixteen arrived wearing a black turtleneck and carrying a silver tray of chai, and he offered a cup to both Diet and me. An older member of the force who looked like a young Saddam Hussein stood up and turned off the soccer game.

I tried not to laugh as I remembered the video of these men attempting jumping jacks. Why had Diet shown me that video? Whenever I am with him, there is something about the polar tension between us that constantly compels both laughter and aggression. I had to pinch myself to keep from laughing as I looked around that room at these men who couldn't pull off a jumping jack, never really considering at the time that maybe the blooper I'd seen on Diet's laptop might have just as much to do with the trainers as the trainees, the monstrous cultural and linguistic gap between the United States and Iraq.

The captain sat down and said something to me. I turned to Rami, who was now seated to my left in his rhinoceros T-shirt.

"He says what do you want to know? He says he will tell you anything."

"Tell me about a day in your life," I said.

"What do you mean?" he asked.

I tried to convey through Rami the nature of my curiosity. I looked at the red, white, and black Iraqi flag behind the captain, the green stars running down the white stripe in the middle. I told Rami to tell the captain that I wanted to know what it was like to be in his shoes. I was always thinking about my father's question: "What about them?" I didn't just want to know about statistics and inventories, the need for electrical upgrades and boots. I wanted the story. I wanted to know what it was like to be a young man training under Diet. I wanted to know what these chai drinkers thought of these dip spitters. I wanted to know what these football fans thought of our kind of football. I wanted to know if there was more to the story of Haditha than the bullet points Diet kept trying to cram down my throat.

The captain held up a pink digital camera in his right hand, a cigarette burning between the fingers of his left, a roll of toilet paper directly in front of me on his desk as a substitute for napkins.

"He says to look at his life," Rami said.

Captain Al'a turned on his camera and beckoned me forward. Just as Diet had wheeled around in his desk chair to show me the training footage, the captain now had something he wanted to show me. He motioned for me to come around the desk.

So I moved closer, deeper into the smell of tobacco and cologne. At first it was confusing and tantalizing as I watched him toggle rapidly through the images of his life. I saw stone houses and white trucks, bright desert days and the faces of friends and images of confiscated or recently purchased weapons atop gravel at night. And then I saw the face of a beautiful Iraqi woman with soft eyes and a white shirt, and she was smiling for the camera, for the captain. The captain shook the camera like dice. He spoke quickly while pointing to the elaborate cabinet on the other side of the room where the black cathode ray tube TV sat beneath a router and a number of other gadgets and knickknacks.

"This is his life," Rami said. "This is the love of his life and their connection is, how do you say—like the computer—like—"

Rami struggled to convey the metaphor. He asked the captain to repeat. The captain gesticulated grandly, sending his arms out wide like a saguaro cactus, now circling the room with the gesture, as if summoning rain or some kind of divine response from the heaven beyond the billowing satin curtains that covered the ceiling.

"Wireless," Rami said. "He says their connection is wireless like the new computers."

The captain seemed just as satisfied as I was with this metaphor. He sat back and rocked in his chair as I tried to gauge the moment. I felt Diet and Moni and my father pushing me in different directions. Was I dropping the ball with all of my questions about haircuts and what it was like to be in the shoes of someone else, all this loosey-goosey empathy bullshit as nothing more than a way for a rookie journalist to dodge the difficult questions of logistics and high-tech weaponry and geopolitical strategy?

"What about them?" my father had asked.

*What about doing your homework and asking a real question?* said the voices of Moni and Diet inside my head, which was really me reminding myself that I was winging it. Dear god. I was always proving myself to someone, every moment of that trip. Every moment of my life. I wanted to drop the name "David Petraeus" just to show that I knew the name. I wanted to hear the captain's opinion on Cheney and Bush and the Al Anbar Awakening and the counterinsurgency strategy and the repercussions of the Haditha massacre, and I wanted to talk about the burn pits and the cancer of the sheikh and his son and all the SEAL complaints about their cowboy desires and the way they conflicted with the Peace Corps–type needs, the way that one guy had said to me that he played *Halo* constantly because he wasn't getting enough kills. Somewhere in that brambled web of context was a great question about this "wireless" connection, but my anxious, slow-witted, rookie disposition couldn't summon the killer rejoinder, so the captain leaned forward and simply showed me another picture.

Inching closer to the captain, I could see the same soft-eyed woman, the love of his life. Only there was a bashfulness and a purple bruise in this shot, the sweet unblemished face now wincing in the light. Thinking about it now, it seems so strange that the captain took, possessed, and shared that photograph with me and that his girlfriend (or wife) posed for it in the first place, but maybe that strangeness was the doorway.

"Sometimes," the captain said, "we do not get along. This is life."

An unsettling telepathy passed between me and the captain in that moment. Or maybe I was the only one who felt it, and maybe the telepathy—that wireless connection—was between me and Karen, ten thousand miles away. I was uncomfortable sitting so close to an openly abusive man on the one hand, but I also felt the tension of his struggle to love someone else and I felt an innocent bond with his desire to openly share across our cultural borders the intimacy of his love life, his wireless connection. Just as every war has a dark side, so does every family and every love story. And we either acknowledge them or we don't.

"I have a wireless connection, too," I said.

The captain's face lit up in that instant. I wanted to ask him for a cigarette so I might share with him some of my story, a day in my life. I wanted to reach out to him like a friend and talk about nights of fights and broken plates and shattered windows and Jack Russell terriers shivering in response to the passion that both fired and burned out my relationship with Karen. But to do so would have been a dereliction of my journalistic duty, or so I told myself. In T. S. Eliot's "The Hollow Men," there is this excruciating stanza about hell as a kind of cowardice:

*Is it like this*
In death's other kingdom
Waking alone
At the hour when we are
Trembling with tenderness
Lips that would kiss
Form prayers to broken stone.

That man had shared one of the most intimate details of his life with me. No American soldier would ever have offered such a photograph to a journalist. Was this one naive and trusting soul reaching out to another? I could have gone further to forge a bond with the captain, but instead I retreated out of fear. This was a man who beat women. End of story. This was no George Washington. This was not the man my father had asked me to find. No, this was a stooge, an ex-thief in a mullet who wore Axe and couldn't do a jumping jack. This was a man who beat his wife. Time to start asking questions about logistics, Matt. Time to straighten up and ask about kidnappings, arrests, timetables, IEDs, and weapons discoveries. Time to gather some facts and statistics. In the end we took another picture in which, again, I'm the only guy smiling.

We returned from the ISWAT compound later that night. Diet stood in front of the dry-erase board in his Conex box and pointed to his barely legible script, his instructions for the stories he wanted me to tell to Americans. He spit dip into an empty water bottle. He looked like a redneck gym teacher during sex ed, so serious and focused. I guess I was his pupil, the guy in the seat dipping with him, his spitting image.

"Okay. You've got the ISWAT team, the civil affairs shit, the school, the human interest, the SEAL mystique, the fifth anniversary. What else? How do you tie them together?"

I told him once again that I didn't need an outline, that I could tell my own story. He gave me a skeptical look, a supercilious smile. Like any good friend, Diet was aware of my fault lines, the fact that I had them. I peed into an empty water bottle, walked my urine over to the door where the other bottles awaited pickup, teased Diet with the prospect of the bottle's warmth against his cheek, something I never would do to a gym coach or a SEAL—or any human being—I did not know. Diet flinched. And then came the lightbulb of an idea in his eyes, as if generated by my puerile transgression. I witnessed what appeared to be the shape of my old high school classmate's prankster smile.

"That bottle of piss is the war in a nutshell," Diet said.

I was prepared to hear his theory, anything to get away from the bullet points on the dry-erase board. It was now quite late at night. I felt like I had seen a lot in my time in Haditha. I had witnessed the burn pit and the ruins of the school. I had spoken to the sheikh and the mayor, and I had conducted two interviews with Captain Al'a, and I kept thinking about how he had described his connection to his girlfriend as "wireless" before showing me the picture of her with that purple bruise on her face. Prior to Diet's lightbulb moment, I kept looking down toward my lap at my black-and-white marbled lab notebook, wondering what to write and what not to write when it came to the captain and Karen and Diet. I kept looking down at Diet's feet, the countless piss-filled bottles lined up like posture-perfect soldiers under hung-up gear. But then he spoke to the elephant in the room. He picked up one of those bottles of piss, as if it were a specimen to be studied in the light. He held it aloft like the Statue of Liberty with her golden torch. I shared in the evaluation of the dark, cidery fluid, what might've passed for an Iraqi black market half liter of gas.

"Nobody really leaves the room anymore," Diet said, looking into the golden glow of his own urine.

He seemed steady as he made this proclamation, full of late-night clarity, the voice of a man who had the experience to speak broadly about not just war, but this war, the Global War on Terror. Diet had done his time. He'd marched on Baghdad and had traveled through Abbottabad, the town where U.S. troops would later find Bin Laden. Diet had built shelters for the Pakistanis in the wake of their devastating earthquake in 2005, and he'd led a special operations force that had brought relative peace to Al Anbar Province, cutting attacks in Haditha from 144 a day to 155 a month, helping to temporarily transform one of the most danger-ous cities in the world. He'd also seen mountains of paperwork and met legions of "fobbits," the men and women who never left the wire of the FOB, the forward operating base, the offices in the desert. He had seen the fobbit sensibility of video game and bored internet surfing, Power-Point presentations and endless masturbation out here—even out here in the wild. He placed that bottle back with the others. He opened a new bottle of water and took a sip, pointed toward the door.

"Out there—where we went today—is the war," he said. "But for 99 percent of the soldiers, *in here* is the war. People pissing in bottles because either one, they're lazy, or two, they're afraid of walking in the dark."

In a matter of hours we would finally walk into the dark.

The next morning I again suggested we take a dip in the Euphrates but was again rebuked with the paternal face, the prankster glint now gone, Diet's eyes looking down over sunglasses and mustache.

"Bad idea, Eat Boy," the look seemed to say.

So, instead of having a swim, I walked over to the plywood gym on the edge of the base, feeling a bit ridiculous as I ran on a treadmill less than a hundred yards from the river. I kept thinking about swimming to the other side, just jumping in the water and floating on over to the KBR contractor camp. But even then it occurred to me that Diet was right to quash this idea. I wasn't yet thinking about the burn pits as the Gulf War syndrome or the Agent Orange of my generation, but I did know that I didn't want to end up with strange growths all over my leg like the sheikh.

While I was doing bench presses, Reynolds dropped by the gym to remind me I was not allowed in the ops hut where Diet was plotting the day's trip—the mission to the desert.

"Just so you know," he said.

Reynolds was just doing his job, but as a member of what some sol-diers referred to as the "Chair Force," he often didn't get much respect. Minutes after he left me alone, Diet knocked on the door of the gym.

"You wanna see what we're doing?"

"Reynolds just said I wasn't allowed."

"I say you're allowed."

I dropped my dumbbells. Diet had a cup of coffee in his hand. We walked through the middle of the camp, the towering Soviet concrete of the Haditha dam looking down on us with the slitted windows of its tenements, a mysterious panopticon staffed by both marines and Iraqis. I cannot tell you all the unverified stories I have heard about what happened in that dam over the course of the war. But I can tell you about one story, because I was able to confirm it, and I will tell that story at the end.

I followed Diet. I stepped into the white trailer, the ops hut. I looked around at his men. Rami was eating one of his legendary tuna sandwiches. Gene the Asian translator was drinking or spitting into a coffee cup. I saw the men who stayed up late playing *Halo*, the ones who were frustrated by all the "Peace Corps bullshit," the fact they weren't getting any kills. I saw the large black man they called Tree and the virtuoso pianist that many of the men suspected to be gay because of his sensitivity to the adopted animals of the base as well as a comment he made one night about the puckered shape of a particular goat's ass.

"Okay," Diet said. "Y'all met Matt. He'll be with us again today. Scotty?"

Diet handed the presentation over to his right-hand man, Scotty, who looked like a mean Tom Hanks. Scotty was from Texas. He seemed to think of Diet as a rich kid from the North and constantly asked me what it was like growing up with him, and at one point I told Scotty a little lie—that his lieutenant once had a baby blue bike with a banana seat, tassels, and bells on the handlebars. It seemed like the sort of detail Scotty was looking for, the kind of dandyish caricature that would confirm his Lone Star stereotypes about us soft and pretty boys from the Northeast.

"First NAI right here," Scotty said, pointing to a coordinate on a PowerPoint map.

"I should probably know this," I said. "But what's an NAI?"

Scotty took an exhausted breath. The only other media personnel this unit had embedded (back in 2007) was Col. Oliver North, a Fox News commentator who was convicted of deceiving Congress, among other things, back in 1988 and later became president of the National Rifle

Association. I was clearly no colonel with Fox News credentials. The paperboy, the friend of the rich lieutenant who rode around on a bicycle with tassels and a bell, had interrupted with yet another question that showed his lack of research. Scotty bugged his eyes and took a withering blink for the other men to register. An NAI was a named area of interest.

"In other words, the bad guys."

That was the plan. We were going to go look for bad guys. Terrorists.

We left the room. Diet made an executive decision. He left Reynolds out of our mission to the desert. It was just us—me and the SEALs. We saddled up with body armor and machine guns, MREs, bottles of water, and SureFire lights. We passed again through the dam, the smell of sulfur and exhaust, the cool breath of the water, the view of the Euphrates to the right, the mechanical bowels beneath us a mere basement of consoles and technicians—or so I believed. What else could be down there?

In my notebook I wrote,

*Gene driving, pass power plant, discarded drums, black bags on barbed wire, tire treads in the yucca, cans, fencing, skeletons of car seats, cinder shards, skulls, bed frames, chest covered in ceramic plate, surefire lights clipped to the side of Gene's helmet.*

We were not fobbits on that day. We drove beyond "the wire," the concrete blocks and bulletproof booths, the HESCO hedges, and spiral rings of concertina. The mood loosened. We were all dipping and spitting, approaching the backside of the dam, Lake Qadisiyah to the left, a body of water that, when viewed from the International Space Station, looks like a coiled sea horse, its hundred kilometers of shoreline appearing no more vast than a river's, but when you're in the desert and all you can see is that water on one side and the desert on the other, the effect is nearly unfathomable. I felt myself to be skirting a great mythic oasis. A mirage. I kept looking for people, for shepherds and warriors, for caravans atop caparisoned camels, Al Qaeda lurking behind every dune with RPGs and bazookas.

Was it true that this was where Saddam's sons buried the young women they raped and killed during the height of the Baathist regime's decadence? How, without GPS, did you know where to go? How did you live out here without billboards and cell towers or even ripraps? Where were the shrubs and grasses, the irrigation canals, the signs of life? How does an NAI, a named area of interest, survive on so little?

"You guys patrol up here often?" I asked.

"The places we're going today we've never been before," Diet said.

I felt my body engorge with adrenaline—fear and desire swimming together. This was the moment I had been waiting for, the moment before the moment, the slow click of the roller coaster as it approaches the peak. I wiped off the lens of my camera repeatedly to preserve the sense of reality, to approximate the vision of someone who was taking pictures outside the vehicle. But this came to seem pathetic. The dust on the window itself was so thick that at one point a picture of the landscape came back as a picture of a camera, the edge of my face. Maybe this was the more accurate shot, the shielded perspective, the inadvertent selfie. Place it right next to Diet's bottles of urine in the museum of us being afraid of them.

There were seven NAIs to visit that day, seven coordinates on a satellite map. The first was a mud hut on the edge of the lake. We came to a stop, that seething wash of silence peppered with radio voices and the hiss of footsteps. I didn't feel like a child but suddenly remembered having once been left in a car on a hot summer day outside a laundromat, unsure if my mother would ever return. As a child, I used to do countdowns to ease my mind, to quell my fear that my mother might never come back. I did countdowns that day in Iraq as I stared at the door handle and looked at my Merrell boots, wondering if I would return home with both legs or at all.

This chanting of numbers must have worked. By the time the soldiers had investigated the empty rooms and the rusty boxes scattered about the sand, I was ready to get out. I wanted to stand up, look into the boxes for myself. I wanted to feel the country. I asked Diet if I could. Like a tentative father, he gave me permission.

I stepped out of the Humvee, felt like the final veil had been removed. Yes, I was finally a man. I'd gone from America to Kuwait to the heavily fortified bases of Baghdad, and from there to the outlying forts and cities to the north. And now today I was beyond all walls, out in the Al Jazira desert with only these men and these vehicles. I was finally in the open, surrounded by the swarming silence of the sands of Babylon, the desert of the Bible. And it felt good. I felt like I'd finally defeated my father, like I was finally, and maybe for the first time in my life, "outside." Forget the International Space Station, Stephen King's metaphor of "the dome," all the scholars who argue that there is no such thing as outside in this transnational surveillance state. Forget all that for a moment, like I did, and feel the awe of the rube snorting his cocaine of war sand, his nitrous of war wind, all that secondhand smoke that seems to have about it a virginal perfume. God, I cannot emphasize enough how delusional and intoxicated I felt in that moment. I remember thinking about Neil Armstrong, who was no relative of mine, but when I was a kid I used to tell people he was my uncle. Yes, I had dreamed of bouncing around on the powdery white berms of the moon. Yes, I was finally living up to the family name, huffing the gas of Iraq, playing soldier with the SEALs. I have never in my life felt more like a man.

But we didn't discover any weapons of mass destruction at that first site. Or the next site. And after a while I started to feel like a boy again, grumpy and sick of his toy, tired of the big day at the museum with all the grownups. We got out of the Humvee and we got back in the Humvee. Over and over. And it was starting to get hot, hard to sit up straight with the weight of my body armor.

About four hours into the mission, as we approached another NAI, the men in my Humvee got into an argument. Diet's music was too sad, according to the other soldiers. Diet disagreed, but his men had serious opinions about music. This was the soundtrack of their lives, their war. They protested for more punk and metal, and so Gene, our driver, plugged in his iPod. Ballads were replaced with power chords and screams, gritty distortion, death metal and hip-hop. We were listening to the vampy voice and the muffled screams of the Canadian electronic feminist, Peaches, "Fuck the Pain Away," when Diet told everyone to "shut the fuck up!"

As we came around a berm, I saw the windows of a mud hut on a hill, a house the color of parchment. There were dark clothes on a line, two red, white, and blue trucks outside. Diet killed the music. After hours of nothing but dunes, this house on the hill was like an apparition. Our lead vehicle was stalled up ahead. I saw a small pond, a wadi, to our left. Our momentum slowed, our tires squealed. And then I began to feel it—we were going down. We began to sink in the Iraqi sand, this fine khaki powder that basically turned to snot when wet.

The proud man turned grumpy boy was now frantic baby. I became afraid, balled my hands into fists. I saw one of our soldiers standing next to the lead vehicle, motioning rather frantically himself with a black fingerless glove while another soldier drew his rifle. Then, I heard a noise in the distance, perhaps the slamming of a door, maybe a gunshot. I saw a figure emerge from the house on the hill and run to the back.

That night before the trip into the desert, just after his speech about the bottles of piss, Diet had toasted my presence in Iraq. We sipped off a flask of care-package bourbon. We talked about women for a while, the ones that got away. As I listened to Diet talk, I kept my notebook in my lap. I kept going back and forth between thinking of him the way I always thought of him—as a friend—and now with this new lens: as the subject of a story yet to be written, a character.

I will return soon to what happened in the desert and everything that happened after, but I need to emphasize the strange thing that happened in Iraq, the way Diet and I both became aware of each other as opposites, poles, roles, characters: Diet and Eat Boy. Big brother and little brother. Conservative and liberal. Destruction and creation. Discipline and gluttony. Warrior and writer. Straight man and fool. We did it to ourselves as teenage boys, but we doubled down on this division, the clarifying fog of the binary, as men. We were the ones who came up with the simple catchy names, and we were the ones who repeated them like some kind of incantation as we grew older. I believe we found great clarity in giving each other these names, Diet and Eat Boy, these seemingly simple roles. But that night before the journey into the desert, after Diet had uttered that humble speech about the bottles of piss as "the story of the war," I started to see the ragged edge of other characters in him, men who lived in the gray. In a few ways it suddenly occurred to me that Diet was unlike anyone I'd ever met but was a bit like men I'd read about in literature. He resembled Fitzgerald's protagonist from *The Great Gatsby*. Like Gatsby (né Gatz), Diet was working class under a glamorous exterior. He was elusive, a man of few words. He would have made a great stunt double for a James Bond lead. Like Gatsby, Diet had left the first love of his life behind, a sweet southern girl we'll call Carrie. Back in those days he often talked of coming home and winning her back, stealing her away from the dentist she'd married, a man we regularly referred to as Dennis. But just as soon as we started to dig into the Carrie story, Diet did what I did to Captain Al'a. On the edge of the gray—the shared bond of a struggle with love—Diet put up a wall. He passed the bottle and asked me again about Karen, the wedding that would never be.

"What really happened?" he said.

"I loved her so much," I said.

Diet gave me face that suggested a bristling relationship with the word "love." If I really did love Karen, why was I in Haditha? Diet and I drank and pissed, laughed and told stories. We were Nick and Gatsby, Sal and Dean, Huck and Jim, Gilgamesh and Enkidu—all these men who chose roads and rivers and wars and deserts over women. But that is of course bullshit—a way of lionizing our lambs, our fears. We were not literary characters. We were real and we were both estranged from the real women of our lives, and once we got on the subject of Karen, it was like we switched roles, flipped character. Diet became the journalist, the one with the penetrating questions.

"You guys still fuck?"

"No," I said.

"You liked fucking a stripper, though, didn't you?"

"Yeah."

"You like the crazy, don't you?"

"Yeah. Just like you."

"You ever still see her?"

I ground my dip into my gums. I felt like I owed Diet the truth. If I wanted him to give me some truth about disaster, maybe I needed to give some disastrous truths back. I'd been unable to do so with Captain Al'a, but here was another chance. My time in Iraq was almost up, and Diet had strayed from his dry-board bullet points and finally seemed ready for the real talk. He had given me the piss theory, which was really just a story about fear, so I tried to confront my fears. I told him about melting down at Gold's Gym and how, on February 28, the very day I'd left for Iraq, just after I'd pulled out of my parking space behind the bookstore of North Carolina A&T, I had received a call. I was on my way to shop for body armor, just hours from my departing flight. I was hoping for a call from my agent and so answered my phone without looking at the number, and instead of my agent with his crisp New Yorker locution, I heard Karen's sobbing voice. As I made the hairpin turn in front of the bookstore where KSM had perhaps purchased engineering textbooks in the 1980s, I heard Karen say, out of nowhere, "I love you."

"Hours away from leaving and she calls to tell me she loves me."

"No," Diet said.

"Yes," I said.

"What did you say?" Diet asked.

"I told her I loved her," I said.

But those words didn't guide me back home to the house with the broken solar panels on the roof. I didn't pull out on my mission to see Iraq. I drove through the neighborhoods where black people live past the uniform yellow one-story houses with clotheslines and past the abandoned war memorial baseball diamond. I topped the rise near Elm Street, Karen's words repeating over and over like a healing balm on top of a wound, like she knew that the trip to Iraq was in no small part a cry, a way of simultaneously announcing and hiding my pain. The only thing bigger and wilder than her love was war, and now that she'd told me that she loved me, part of me felt that I didn't actually need to go, that I'd passed the test, that my hunger for war was really nothing of the kind but instead some kind of suicidal dare to the illusion of love. I tried to convey this to Diet, but I don't think I succeeded in illustrating how strange that drive was on my way to Southern Firearms, that feeling I had for a brief unforgettable moment like I was choosing this—guns and violence and war—Diet himself—over love.

Diet mercifully did not ask me to go further with that story. So I never told him about walking into the gun shop feeling like a zombie, hypnotized by war, the bizarre feeling of joining some strange, secret club as I stared at pistols and assault rifles and burnt orange vests, boxes of buckshot, photos of dead deer, Glocks under glass. I never told Diet how I felt like the Hollywood ending was within my grasp, this whole idea of spring break in Iraq as just one big bluff to win back Karen's love, a last-ditch ploy to show how wild and serious my love for her was. I never confessed that I had in a way chosen our friendship over reconciliation with Karen. What I did say was this: "I feel like I see Karen's ghost every-where. I think about her all the time."

If Diet was Gatsby, who was I? Nick Carraway? From a certain dis-tance, the comparison sheds a little light—Diet the active and Eat Boy the passive, Diet the hero and Eat Boy the apostle, Nick so determined to withhold judgment on the world due to the fog of privilege his father warns him about when he's younger, Diet the one who pulled himself up by his bootstraps. But the simple truth is that Diet and I were not characters. We may be here and now on this page, but we were and are more than that, and less. We were both haunted with the ghosts of the women we loved, yes, but also with the ghost of each other, these char-acters we'd turned ourselves into: Diet and Eat Boy.

Diet passed me the bottle. It felt good to wash away self-conscious sentiments with rich, honeyed belts of bourbon. The conversation moved on from symbolic bottles of piss and overwrought memories of Karen to lighter fare. The Grateful Dead—"Dark Star" from the 1969 album *Live/ Dead*—played low on Diet's MacBook as we talked about our best friends from high school (and even further back) and the things we'd all done together and how remarkable it was that we were all still friends. We had all made a pilgrimage to see the Dead together in 1995, right before Jerry Garcia died. It was one of the many experiences that had consecrated our friendship. I had sent Diet a bootleg of that show his first year in the Naval Academy. So to hear that particular music in Iraq was meaningful, I suspect, to both of us.

"I'm getting some good stuff," I told him. "I think I'm starting to see the story."

"Just don't sell out," Diet said. "Don't be one of these writers who just writes about the most dramatic shit. I've heard your questions. There's more to this place than just the Haditha massacre."

"I know that," I said. "But that doesn't mean you can just ignore it. It's called context."

"That was a long time ago. That was one fucking day."

"It was just a couple years ago," I said. "I imagine the Hadithans haven't forgotten."

"I just know you," Diet said. "I've read your stuff. You like the dramatic."

"So do you," I said. "That's why you're here."

"You know what I mean."

"Nobody has been held accountable for that day," I said. "And that's part of the story of this war: Accountability. War crimes. The first three years."

"What are you talking about, war crimes?"

"What am I talking about? I don't know—Geneva Conventions? Torture? Assassinations? Illegal invasion? Abu Ghraib? The extraordinary rendition program? Dick Cheney? The dark side? The fact that Iraq had nothing to do with 9/11 but here we are?"

"Come on. That's all bullshit."

"This war is bullshit, and it's fucking criminal."

"Dude, I wanna hit you so bad right now."

Things changed just like that. The bourbon giveth and the bourbon taketh away. One second we're basking in the warm swarm of the Grateful Dead and the next we're on the edge of our seats, and I could tell by the way Diet was shaking that he was telling the truth—that he did want to hit me. There were dark shreds of dip spilling out of the side of his mouth, like his mustache was coming undone, or maybe I'm wrong. Maybe it only appeared like he was shaking because I was shaking. I felt like Karen during one of our many fights. I actually wanted Diet to hit me, wanted to feel the words explode into action.

But how to compare the danger of a conversation with that day in the desert, our vehicles suddenly stranded in the mud, mysterious figures in black spilling out of the house on the hill, several SEALS now marching, with their machine guns poised, toward this strange outpost in the middle of nowhere.

"Don't put this picture in the paper," said a soldier standing in the turret of one of the sinking Humvees.

But I took that quagmire shot, what became a front-page image in the *Winchester Star* a month later. I then put my camera away and helped dig out the Humvee's tires with a shovel, feeling simultaneously like a traitor and part of the team. I moved with a fear and speed I'd never known. I turned around at one point to get my breath, to see the soldiers with their guns, to see if the people on the hill had weapons of their own. I saw a black-hooded figure moving across the desert with a cinched pile of sticks atop her head. In the east I saw two other figures, two shepherds, leading a flock of about fifty sheep over a hill toward the pond on our left, and I wondered if these figures were harbingers of death, the sheep like the coming clouds of heaven. I felt like I was in a scene from a myth, like maybe I was creating a myth to ward off my fear of death. The world seemed ablaze with significance.

The features of the shepherds resolved on the horizon. I could now see: they were children. One of them wore a long white shirt, and the other, the shorter one, wore what looked to be an American hand-me-down, a light green jersey with blue racing stripes and the number fifty-five. I began to feel like maybe, just maybe, these strangers were not evil. Had the shepherds been adults, this fundamental realization may have never dawned on me and I might have continued to bristle with fear, but when I saw that the shepherds were children and that they were walking toward us, I began to walk toward them. I met them at the edge of the water, the wadi. They were the first unplotted characters of the trip, the first Iraqis I'd met outside the context of the wire, the base. For an unforgettable instant, it was just the three of us.

"Give? Give?"

I think about this moment all the time, this unplanned meeting of strangers and this single English word between us. They held out their hands, looked left and right, that word—*give*—always uttered with that upturned inflection, always a question. Diet walked over to join us. He tried out his Arabic. I tried out mine. The boys held each other's hands while we peppered them with questions.

Salah, the translator who had helped me interview the sheikh whose leg and whose son were riddled with cancer, joined us at the edge of the pond, where I could see a watery reflection of Diet with his hands wheeling in the air like he was conjuring a magic trick for the kids. I remember seeing the bleached and crumpled cardboard remains of an MRE at my

feet, wondering for a moment if Diet had lied to me, if he and his men
had been here before, or if they hadn't, then what soldiers had preceded
the SEALs with these rations? That MRE was a discrepancy. How did this
particular piece of American garbage arrive? How did this American T-shirt
with the number fifty-five end up on the back of this boy whose name
was the same as the boy I'd met in the ruins of the girls' school: Faris.

I examined the child's used American jersey, the number fifty-five. His
cracked palms jabbed at the air, this Iraqi child who would grow up with
memories of Americans suddenly appearing like mirages in the desert.
I felt overwhelmed, helpless in every way. On the one hand, we didn't
know if we were about to be attacked by his family, but that was not the
real fear. The real source of my growing anxiety was that I had virtually
nothing to give to these children who kept saying, "Give? Give?"

I took out a blue paisley handkerchief. It was still new, not yet stained
with my sweat. Before I'd left for Iraq I'd stood in front of a mirror at an
outdoor store and tried it on, imagining myself as a soldier in that moment,
a guy with a shaved head and that badass biker look, that suggestion of
the pirate and the rock star, the Blackwater contractor before Blackwater
got exposed and disappeared. When I handed it over, Faris smiled. His
brother, whose name was Sahat, continued to say "Give." He started tugging enviously at the handkerchief, souring the features of his brother.
Diet smiled and shook his head. I dug into my pack and gave the other
brother a single American dollar.

"Shukran," he said, meaning "thank you."

"Good boy, Eat Boy," Diet said.

Diet walked away, talked into his headset, pointed at the house on
the hill. I stood with the two children and the translator, surrounded by
sheep. We watched as the Humvees winched each other from the mud.
Back in the vehicle, moments later, I would find out that the people on
the hill were not terrorists. They were relatives of Captain Al'a, the Axe-
soaked leader of the SEAL-trained SWAT team, the mulleted man I'd met
on my first night in Haditha, the one who felt that "wireless" connection
with his girlfriend. This fact felt nearly magical, that full-circle storytelling
resonance, like Moni telling me that the mastermind of 9/11 had been
educated in my own backyard.

I took out my notebook. I made small talk with Salah. I asked him the fundamental question Moni had asked me: "Who do you work for?"

He just smiled at first. This is an important question, I now know—this establishment of tribe. I was not just with a SEAL unit. I was with a JSOF unit, a Joint Special Operations Force, emphasis on the word "Joint." JSOFs are like all-star teams or maybe more like celebrity golf tournaments. They're made of SEALs, rangers, marines, and all kinds of contractors. When Salah refused to answer my question, I pressed, feeling like Moni, imagining myself as Moni.

"Private sector?" I asked.

"Big company," Salah said.

"Big company?" I said.

"You know the name," he said.

I responded with a genuinely naive smile.

"Come on," he said. "CIA."

After I wrote down that conversation right there in the moment, one of the gunners, a man who is now dead, stood in his turret and threw peaches from a can into my mouth, inspiring other men to dance around like hungry tigers on their hind feet—the lighter side of Operation Iraqi Freedom. Standing there, in what was ostensibly the front yard of Captain Al'a's cousins, I felt like I was at a barbecue. We were all friends. Through Al'a, these Iraqis knew who we were. Tom Byrd might have pulled out on sponsoring my trip to Iraq, but there was no way he would be able to resist the good news I'd found. The essence of my story for the *Winchester Star* would be this: look at the good work of our hometown boy and the American soldiers. In the middle of the desert our reputation preceded us. Because of the work of my friend—the lieutenant—what might have been an insurgent outpost in the past was now a home where the American flag was welcomed. Because we took the time to work with this man, we were welcomed by his family, these people who lived in this humble hut on this hill in the middle of nowhere. I gave the editors that quagmire picture of the Humvee sinking in the sand, but I didn't tell them to run it as some emblematic front-page shot. When they did, it surprised me and pissed Diet off. But I don't own this story, and neither does Diet.

After the encounter with the cousins of Captain Al'a, we drove on until sunset, at which point we stepped out of our Humvees under a darkening sky. We pissed in the sand. I was starting to like these guys, to believe they were nothing more—or less—than good, hardworking men doing the best they could in circumstances beyond their control. They too were victims of the war on terror, the agendas of old men. The sky turned black. The green night vision goggles came on. We navigated by satellite imagery, wireless communication. We were the blue dots. The Iraqis were the reds. We approached a hut.

I wrote in my notebook:

*Nighttime. Write by red light. Fleer telescope camera. Patrolling the desert. Boats on the lake. Planes coming. Boys spitting and listening. Stars as outdated coordinates outside dusty window. Blue dots are us. Green goggles for them. Fires on the hill. Probably humble herders but I'm back in the truck cuz I don't know. Orion has more chainmail than I've ever seen. Groin of the gunner in the iPod light.*

We knew from our satellite imagery that there were people inside the hut. We walked in the dark with guns drawn, knocked on the door. The door opened. We entered the mud brick home of a group of fishermen with wizened faces and iron beds, several still arrayed in a semicircle on a handwoven brown prayer rug, seven men and a boy with faces lit by a Coleman lantern, shoes at the door. One of them smiled at us and seemed to tell us his story.

I wrote in my notebook:

*Man with two wives, one on each side of the river, staying alone in a stone hut with a gas lamp, taking a month to fish, says he doesn't want his children to "get hooked on fishing," wants them to get degrees, but there aren't any jobs. Has a rod, a shotgun, clothes on hooks, food on a wooden window shelf, cooler of water, and a single iron bed strewn with clothes, blankets. Member of the Zawi tribe.*

I wrote down the Arabic word for home: *baitee.*

"The American people must decide," the man said. "We just want peace and quiet."

If this were a novel, here would be the place for the grenade, the flash of a Kalashnikov. I once taught Don DeLillo's *White Noise* to a class of first-year college students, and when one of them said to me, "I kept waiting for someone to die so I would know what it all means," I understood what she was saying. I have known that strange editor inside who wants people—characters—to die, and maybe this is the same part of us that sends our friends and children to war and watches the news until we can no longer watch the news. But luckily for me and my friend, the IED or the grenade or the gunshot never came. The Iraqis just seemed to want to talk to us, and as I listened to the music of their language and listened to Diet and Salah and the other men try to play along, their faces occasionally cracking with a glint of wit, something broke in me. It's a difficult thing to recall while buoyed by the safety of this country and this caffeine and this office that is also my home, but I remember feeling it in my entire body, my own fatigue filling me with a sudden pride in my friend. Five years deep into the "forever war" and Diet and his men weren't kicking down doors, honoring their own desire for "more kills" so they could know what it all means. Instead, they were knocking. They were speaking Arabic. After the disasters of Abu Ghraib and the Haditha massacre just miles away, here they were, embodying the answer to my father's question, seeking those men—those heroes—themselves, and not as journalists, but as partners and neighbors.

"But what about them?" my father asked.

I think it's fair to say that some Americans tried to shatter that illusion of a border, a wall, that line between "us" and "them." We all know what came later, with Iraq descending into chaos after the American withdrawal and the reign of ISIS, but in between that possibly criminal invasion of 2003 by our country and the takeover by ISIS ten years later, there were men like my friend who tried "to clean up the mess," and they did so by building relationships with Iraqis that were so strong that when they found their vehicles sinking in the sand in the middle of the Al Jazira desert, they had nothing to fear because the strangers on the hill weren't strangers at all. Don't worry, reader. Someone will die in this book. We will confront that universal mystery. But the power of what had *not* happened that day washed over me in that fishermen's hut. We were alive because of Captain Al'a and the way Diet and his men had forged a friendship with this man who had lost nearly half of his family to war.

I looked at my friend, at work in the dark, so far away from home, and I wanted to pat him on the back, give him a hug. I wanted to take a picture of the smiling fishermen and the smiling soldiers, but some part of me was starting to cave. The larger part of me didn't want to take a picture. I just wanted to witness. I wanted to listen to Americans speaking Arabic.

After about a half hour of conversation, the fishermen wished peace upon us and we wished peace upon them. We returned to the Humvees. Which is to say, we never met resistance in the desert that day, that night. Al Qaeda and their WMDs were nowhere to be found. We drove on and on, listening to rock and roll, country, hip-hop, and silence. Some nights these patrols would last for so long that Diet claimed he and his men would hallucinate, see clowns and cowboys. After that particular mission was done—after we passed again through the bowels of the dam—I once again, as if intoxicated by a death wish, suggested a swim in the Euphrates but was once again greeted with looks, with comments about my skin falling off.

It was time to sleep. I thought of the shepherds and their flocks of sheep. I thought of the good feeling of hearing Diet's men cheering as I caught that peach. I thought of the sheikh, all the people downstream. The most important story from my time in Iraq may well have been the quietest, the sound of a distant fire at night, ashes swirling in front of stars, the burn pits, the sound of polluted soil slipping into Euphrates silt and feeding the flowers and dates and goats and eventual stomachs of the folks just around the bend where the palm trees grow, that lush moment of riverbank greenery perhaps an illusion of health, all the friendships our soldiers were building undercut by the fires our contractors were burning. The burn pits were run by a mysterious corporation that slept on the other side of the river, and these men did more than just burn trash. Sometimes they, like me, saw mysterious things they weren't supposed to and were sworn to secrecy for having seen those things. But sometimes the things they saw were so infuriating that they just couldn't help themselves. They had to tell their stories.

# 8. FEBRUARY 2008

## AMERICA AND KUWAIT

I love my country. I don't trust my
government.

—GRAFFITI FROM THE WAR

Once I had launched my mission to see Iraq for myself, accomplishing it
became the only thing I could think about. When the *Winchester Star*
withdrew its sponsorship, I felt split: one part despair, one part desire. As
the holidays approached, I didn't know which part would win out, but
I did everything in my power to avoid feeling powerless. I obsessed. I
drank. I screamed. I prayed. I lifted weights. I ran. I wrote. I told strangers
I was about to embed with SEALs. I told my students. Fake it until you
make it, as they say in AA. Yes, I pretended as if I were going to Iraq. I told
everyone I knew that I was going, as if there were some great beneficial
pressure to be gained from the announcement, the expectancy growing
in the eyes of my world. I took furious, oblivious notes. I constructed lists.
I checked the boxes in the emails the military sent me. They told me I
needed body armor, and not just any old body armor. I needed ceramic
plates. And in light of a recent typhoid epidemic, I needed vaccinations.
I needed my electronic initials all over the place to let the military know
that I knew that they owed me nothing in the event of a kidnapping or
killing. I had to sign a "hold harmless" agreement. I had to sign off on
their media ground rules. I needed to be aware that if I did complete all
my paperwork and I did purchase a ticket to Kuwait, that the military

would fly me to Baghdad prior to my embed, and it was there that they would take my biometrics, that is, read my eyes and scan my ocular prints into a computer, where they would remain for a certain period of time, perhaps indefinitely. Was I being lured into giving my identity to Big Brother and his friends inside the matrix? How would the story behind the story haunt me in the years to come?

Shortly after the Christmas holiday, I received a letter about an upcoming literary conference in New York City, something called AWP (Association of Writers & Writing Programs). The letter gave me an idea. I jumped in the kitchen. I did pistons. I was a human pogo stick witnessed only by the dogs of my roommate. Here was the idea: Earlier that year Kevin Rippin (the penguin-shaped poet) and I had tossed back a bottle of wine at his house. At the end of the night, after workshopping some poetry, we spent some time bashing our department. We were particularly incensed over our dean's recent demand that we start gearing our scholarship in an "interdisciplinary" direction. In spite of the lofty rhetoric that often accompanied conversations about interdisciplinarity, many of us believed interdisciplinary scholarship was, nine times out of ten, an excuse for flaccid, general discussions in place of specific, rigorous research or, in our case, compelling fiction and poetry, the kind of stuff people read out loud at AWP. Be that as it may, Rip and I both agreed that night that there might be one way to use this "interdisciplinary" mandate as a Trojan horse for fiction and poetry. What if we created a literary journal but called it interdisciplinary? We could throw in a few token pieces of research, but it would be primarily a magazine for literature. We even came up with a name: *Convergence Quarterly*.

"I have an idea," I told Rip at the office right after Christmas break.

"Oh, shit, Matty's got an idea," he said.

Rip was wearing one of his famously ornate sweaters, a silver-and-black number with a pattern so dense and dizzying it almost made me vomit. We stepped outside so he could smoke, so none of our colleagues would overhear. For the first time I began to see the metaphoric quality of the enterprise I was about to embark upon. Yes, it partially occurred to me that my journey into the Muslim world might have to run a path parallel to that of my Christian president, that I might have to conspire secretly with my colleagues and perhaps shift my justification-slash-rationale as I went. If the *Winchester Star* wouldn't sponsor me, *Convergence Quarterly* (what would ultimately become *Convergence Review*) would have to do.

"We haven't even put out a fucking issue," Rip said.

"Doesn't matter," I said.

"Doesn't matter? Matty, we could go to jail for this."

"Not if we actually make the magazine," I said. "I just need somebody legitimate to write me a letter of accreditation. I need an editor. I need you."

"We're not fucking legitimate, Matty. We haven't done jack fucking shit."

"So let's get legitimate. Let's start," I said.

"I'm not going to fucking jail," Rip said.

I had a sudden vision of myself as an ersatz George W. Bush imprisoned for faking his way into Iraq, a white American idiot in an orange jumpsuit giving interviews to more intelligent writers, the American idiot making thundering declarations on camera, the American idiot adjusting his glasses for Larry King, the American idiot in his Gitmo jumpsuit chastising his country for throwing writers and whistle-blowers—truth-tellers—in prison while the true criminals, the politicians and bankers, played golf.

Rip seemed worried about the law and getting thrown under the bus if things didn't work out. Like my father, he had the prospect of beheadings haunting his thoughts. He was shaking his head a lot, swishing his tongue around behind his lower lip, digging his hands into his pockets, looking furtively around as if the NSA might be listening to us. Rip had a wife and a dog and aging parents in Johnstown whom he loved. He had a mortgage.

"Look," I said. "If you'll be my editor and just write me a letter, I will not only owe you big, I promise you: we will make the magazine. Even if I have to fund it by going into credit card debt. It'll be legitimate, Rip. I promise. And it could be good. Think about it. We might have fun with it, and it might actually succeed."

"Matty, I'm not going to have any fun with it if you're fucking dead," Rip said.

Rip's face recoiled as he spoke those words. I came down out of the clouds. I was touched. I didn't know what to say. I could tell that Rip

cared about me. I bummed a cigarette. I'll never forget that cigarette, the
looks we shared during the silent space of that smoke break, the dead,
torn-up grass of the flag football field in front of our office like the war
zone in my brain we were both about to populate.

"Motherfucker," Rip said.

"What?" I said.

"I wish I was going with you," he said.

I took two trips in the two months before I got on the plane for Kuwait:
one to Naples, Florida, and one to New York City for that literary conference. I traveled to Naples because my grandfather lived there and he
was dying. I loved that man I called Bumpa. My father called him Pop.
Bumpa was an engineer who had graduated from the University of Michigan and was recruited to design the bellows for the atomic bomb. My
brother, Andy, in an act of innocent citizen journalism, had discovered
through a high school interview project something my father knew. Bumpa
was a part of the Manhattan Project, a chapter of American history that
continues to haunt us to this day. Back in the nineties my brother had
captured on home video the story of Bumpa's involvement with America's WMDs. How strange this all seems now. After all, we invaded Iraq
to find WMDs and we sanctioned Iran to keep them from developing
WMDs, but there's only one country in the history of the world to ever
use a nuclear weapon on another country, and my grandfather helped
design that weapon. He was a member of the so-called Greatest Generation, the hard and stoic stock of mid-twentieth-century Americans who
defeated the forces of foreign fascism on the one hand but also rounded
up "Japs" into concentration camps on the other. He came from an America that built great highways and put a man on the moon but also an
America that told women to shut up and firebombed Japanese cities to
smithereens, killing a hundred thousand civilians a night at the peak of
World War II. Bumpa was ninety-three that January of my visit, living
in a plush retirement community called Bentley Village, and the simple
fact is I didn't want him to die.

My sister and I sat in the backseat of a white Malibu rental as we
wound our way past palm trees and bougainvillea and putting greens,

octogenarians, many of them smiling and waving, slowly negotiating speed bumps behind the zippered plastic windows of golf carts. My father and mother were in the front seat. It was the middle of the afternoon. We all knew that this was quite likely the last time we'd get to see this man whom we all loved so much.

We parked the car in the visitors' lot, close to the carport where my grandfather's white Cadillac sat. We walked toward an Astroturfed stairwell. I remember feeling lucky and young, bounding up the steps. Then, waiting for my parents, I felt not only the heaviness of my own heart, but a strong sense of my father's. I put a hand on his shoulder as we waited at Bumpa's door. I wanted that hand to communicate to my father that I felt his pain and that, for whatever it was worth, I was on his side.

I felt no more resentment for my father's attempt at derailing my plans for Iraq. On the contrary, I felt a wave of doubt that day, the proximity of my grandfather's death and my mother's sickness and the feeling of love and family all around me lacing my writerly detachment and certitude with a sense that everything that I thought was really important was nothing more than vanity.

Bumpa answered the door. He had a white mustache, his scalp red and ravaged, his nose a burned beak bearing the signs of a million days under the twentieth-century sun, years of hockey on the frozen Michigan lake of his old backyard. He used to be a six-footer, but he'd now shrunk down to about five nine. There was a wheezy stutter in his breathing I'd never heard before. But there was still that sly corner-of-the-mouth smile of the guy who loved jokes and playing poker. He hugged us all in the doorway to his apartment and invited us in, a painting of his old Michigan lakefront home on the hallway wall, Carolyn, his sixty-year-old girlfriend, standing at his side, the smell in that apartment a cross between a baby's room and a barbershop, that sense of old man powdery scalp mingling with the sweet, Metamucil-laced scent of a laxative-induced dump, a not so subtle cinnamon potpourri sprinkled on top.

"How are you, Pop?" my father asked.

Bumpa blew out his cheeks and bugged his eyes to answer that question. My sister and I exchanged baleful looks. I think we were both on the verge of crying. Bumpa used to call my sister "Bobby Boy" because of how short she used to wear her hair when she was a tomboy toddler who could outrun all the boys in her class (and mine). God, we loved that man so much. But we all knew the end was near. Many of Bumpa's things were in boxes. Carolyn turned down the TV, the performance of an opera. We all took seats in the living room.

I want to say so many things about my grandfather, but for the purposes of this story I just need to share a couple. My grandfather believed in me. He believed in my dream of being a writer. When Carolyn's schizophrenic son, Doug, moved his pup tent onto the lawn of the double-wide trailer Bumpa had bought for her at the beginning of their relationship, Bumpa made a point of sneaking into Doug's tent and stealing his journals and sending copies to me so I could get a clear picture of the schizophrenic mind for a novel I was working on called *Schizo*. At eighty-six Bumpa flew to Virginia for my college graduation. After I'd received an award for being James Madison University's "history student of the year," he told me, "Keep doing what you're doing. You're doing good."

He was a man of few words, but when Bumpa offered encouragement, he meant it, and therefore you felt it. I always admired my father because he had chosen a different path than his father, and I wanted my father to see that same spirit in me, my desire to be a writer not some oedipal rejection of him but my own way of honoring his path, the way he'd struck out on his own.

From what my father tells me, growing up with my grandfather wasn't always easy. Bumpa was often cold and quiet, with a hair-trigger temper, a face that could go blood red in a heartbeat. My grandmother, whose name was Zora but whom we called Gaum, often felt alone in her marriage, and my father saw this. He felt her pain.

"Before it became fashionable, she used to always talk about the 'military industrial complex,'" my father told me. "She was a very smart woman. She never got a college degree, but she read every book she could get her hands on."

My father did the same, perhaps one of his subtle tributes to his mother, perhaps one of the ways he, too, dealt with loneliness, that sense of something missing. I never got to see that erudite side of my grandmother, that critical and lively curiosity. But I felt the echo in my father and beyond.

After Gaum died of Alzheimer's in 1992, Bumpa began to thaw, as if her exit had also been her entry. Bumpa started to come out of his shell, to ask questions. That day in his apartment I heard more words come out of his mouth than I'd ever heard before, the presence of death perhaps the storyteller's best friend.

It all seemed to start with a shave, a self-consciousness about hair. After some awkward small talk, Bumpa announced to my father that he wanted to get rid of his mustache. I think he wanted to see his face one more time. So my dad put a towel around Bumpa's shoulders and went to work, trimmed around his neck and head while my sister and I rummaged through boxes of photographs. Sitting down at one point at the kitchen table, watching my father clip away, I could see them both relax, father and son. Carolyn, a squatty woman with silver shoulder-length hair, put on a pot of coffee and brought out Bumpa's nose clippers at my father's request. He had four of them—four different razors just for his nose. My mother and I playfully began to use them. It was a big, funny grooming party for a moment, everybody wielding and marveling at the different varieties of clippers, everybody looking at each other's nose hairs, my mother cackling, Carolyn pouring coffee and fixing everybody up with a scoop of vanilla ice cream, Bumpa seeming more and more comfortable, more alert, more alive, like he was coming back to life, not leaving it behind.

After the haircut and after he'd finished his sundae and coffee, he started to talk. I don't remember exactly where the story began, but at one point he started reminiscing about Michigan, the old homes he'd lived in, the house on Gilbert Lake, the other on Strawberry Lake, the house on Greenview with the rock pond. My father brought up an anecdote of his own, a day when he was sixteen and he'd accidentally driven the family car right through the garage door. Bumpa smiled, blinked rapidly, his shaved face a revelation to me, like a time traveler's glimpse at the young man—the soft-faced, sensitive boy my grandfather once was.

"When I was six years old, one of our neighbors had just purchased a Model A," Bumpa said. "He came home one day, honking the horn. I ran out to the street, asked him if I could park it for him. He asked me if I knew how to drive. I said, 'Sure, I can drive.' I just didn't know how to brake!"

He bugged his eyes to accentuate the punch line. My six-year-old grandfather had driven his neighbor's Model A through the garage and right out the back, coming to a muddy, smoking stop in the guy's backyard. We all howled with laughter. Bumpa smiled.

"I had never heard that story before," my mother exclaimed as we drove home.

"I hadn't either," my dad said.

Somehow my grandfather had managed to hold a story back until the end, a secret tale of mischief that reached across the decades to connect with the story of his son. Back at our condo that night, we went through the boxes of Bumpa's things before bed, trying to decide what to throw out and what to keep. Who wanted a pastel-green smoker jacket, a loud pair of floral printed pants? Who wanted a wooden driver or a silver tracksuit? I nearly tossed to the garbage a cheap mesh University of Michigan baseball hat, but on the underside of the brim I felt a lump. There was something hidden under the tight blue fabric, something hard and square. I grabbed a steak knife from the kitchen and cut into the cloth and removed a beige piece of plastic. I pried open the plastic and found what appeared to be a primitive green microchip inside, copper wires forming vectory paths toward silver nodes. I marched into my parents' bedroom.

"Quick question," I said. "What the hell is this?"

This is a story about secrets: the known unknowns and the unknown unknowns, family and self and country and world coming to light in the strangest and most common private moments. How well do you know what's in your own backyard? What are you willing to put on the table to break down the walls before it's too late?

"Was Bumpa a spy?" I asked.

My mother gave me an indulgent look, never wanting to dismiss her son's thoughts. My dad, on the other hand, struck a more skeptical face, like he'd just discovered a bone in a piece of fish. He held the device in his hand, turned it over several times.

"It looks like a bug," I said.

"It's not a bug," my dad said.

"Then what is it?"

"You are becoming way too paranoid," he said.

"Wonder why," I said.

My mother laughed at that and made one of her famous tisking sounds. My father suggested we take a walk before bed. Our condo was in a gated community, a series of white duplexes and fountain-rippled ponds skirting a premier international tennis club that was about to get gutted by the recession. But that night, walking the dark paved road that rimmed the development—a wall of pines to our right, the manicured lawns and grapefruit trees and luxury cars of our neighbors to our left—there was no sense of economic doom. Our impending apocalypse was a more personal thing. My mother and my grandfather were dying.

The street artist Banksy once wrote, "Your mind is working at its best when you're being paranoid. You explore every avenue and possibility of your situation at high speed with total clarity." I'm not sure about the "total clarity" part, but I think my father and I were both in a pretty exploratory space that night, and although we were somewhat fueled by fear, we were also firmly aware of our love for each other. After a few small-talk observations about the beauty of the trees and the stars, I told him,

"I'm going to Iraq, Dad. It's official."

"You're really going to do it?" he said.

"The paperwork's in place," I said. "I've got a literary journal that's going to sponsor me."

My father, who has always been a big reader, was nevertheless prompted to produce a withering wince by the mention of a "literary journal." But something had finally changed between us or maybe he was just in an accepting mood that night, perhaps reminded by his own father of just how difficult it is to be the son of an Armstrong father.

"Okay," he said. "So what are you going to write about when you get over there?"

"I won't know until I get there."

"Sure, but you need a plan. What are you looking for?"

This was a good question. I didn't know the answer. All I knew was what I'd read: Haditha was in Al Anbar Province, and apparently there was something going on called the "Al Anbar Awakening." The insurgents were apparently starting to work with the Americans. The Haditha massacre was in the past. Charges were being brought. Violence was going down. There was talk of a handoff, a lot of excitement about Gen. David Petraeus and his theory of counterinsurgency. Some thought Petraeus a genius, while others thought his "theory" boiled down to nothing more than dollar diplomacy—soldiers handing out wads of cash to keep Iraqis quiet until Americans could make a respectable exit, Vietnam style. I more or less summarized these talking points to my father as we strolled past SUVs and the blinking blue light of Florida retirees watching late-night TV.

"What about *them?*" my father asked.

I will be forever grateful for my father's curiosity, the way he set his fears aside to express his love, his final acceptance. His intervention had failed. His desire to keep the regime of my mind from changing had been thwarted. So he was now digging in to help me in the only way he could: he was putting himself in my shoes, pretending to be the young writer with the assignment of his life, his first trip to a war zone.

"What do you mean, 'what about them?'" I said.

"I mean you want to tell a unique story, something nobody's heard before. Everything I read about this war seems to be about us, and all the bad news. But what about *them?* Are there any Iraqi heroes cropping up? Who's their good guy? Who's their George Washington?"

My father loved patriotic history, stories of the American Revolution and the founding fathers. So did I. I was proud of the way we'd defeated our imperial masters and an increasingly crazy king. But my father's advice about finding the Iraqi revolutionaries has led me to some strange and mysterious discoveries. It was my father who first put the bug in my ear, the notion that maybe there were heroes among our enemies and that maybe the "terrorists" were a bit like us: revolutionaries, people who wanted freedom from oppression. Human beings.

We turned around at a cul-de-sac, waved to an elderly woman walking a white dog. We were quiet for a while, taking in the stars and the warm breeze.

"Do you ever hear from Karen?" he asked.

"I see her at the gym sometimes," I said.

I didn't want to say any more than that, didn't feel like spilling my guts about how I'd more or less threatened suicide. Part of me thought my father already knew about this, that Andy had probably told him. But even if this were true, I also felt as if I could communicate a kind of stability and sanity to my father by showing that I was capable of brushing aside his question, by not descending into a torrent of tears and self-doubt.

My father didn't press me about Karen, and so I didn't press him about his father, my suspicions about our family's history and our role in the development of the only nuclear weapons ever used on another country. Yes, before I smoked pot out of a bong named after the *Enola Gay*, my grandfather had helped develop the very bombs the *Enola Gay* would drop on Japan.

I tried to forget the strange device in my grandfather's hat. I stared up at the Florida stars, wondered how they'd look in Iraq. I tried to enjoy the end of my walk with my father, the opulent landscaping, the glisten of the sprinklered water on the crabgrass, the nocturnal lime trees, the fleur-de-lis fountain in the pond behind our condo, the furtive lizards on the white slab steps leading up to our back door, the splendor of this gated community. I gave my father a hug. I told him I loved him. Two weeks later and I was behind another kind of gate, staring into the gaping cavity of Ground Zero.

After the towers fell and before the Freedom Tower rose from the ashes, there was a hole in the ground in the middle of New York City. Here was the first burn pit of the Global War on Terror. Here was the first site of attack by the mastermind, the one they called KSM. For many Americans, here was why we destroyed Iraq and destabilized the entire Middle East. Across the street from an old eighteenth-century iron-gated church with a grassy graveyard, I stood facing what was now a new kind of graveyard: Ground Zero.

"If you see something, say something" instructed a sign on the nearby fence.

"Winter clearance," announced another.

That really struck me, the winter clearance thing, because that's what I saw as I looked out on what was once a great symbol of American power. As a child I'd taken the elevator to the top of the twin towers and felt my ears pop, and I'd looked down at the taxicabs speeding like Pac-Men through the lanes of the city. I'd felt a strange strong wind at the base of those buildings, a foreboding sense of the suicidal energy I toyed with once we reached the top of that concrete filing cabinet, that Superman desire to jump, to see if maybe, just maybe, an act of faith might be the key to learning how to fly.

But now the towers were gone.

Winter clearance.

Nothing left now but a gutted and gridded hole, kids climbing concrete blocks to peer over the cyclone fence screen into the cavity, like they half-expected to see a ballgame, a field of green. I heard a homeless man fluting out the notes to "Amazing Grace," a jackhammer backing him up with its relentless percussion.

It was a cold, clear February day, the stock market plunge still months away. I stood on Broadway, staring at the cross on the roof of St. Paul's Church, remembering the photo of the twin towers in the fog looming over this very same cross on the cover of one of my favorite novels, Don DeLillo's *Underworld*. I was in New York for a writers' conference, killing some time walking the streets, waiting for a phone call from an old girlfriend named Catherine who now lived in the Park Slope section of Brooklyn. For the first time in my life, I had a cell phone in my pocket. Yes, the country rube was stalking the city streets with his new flip phone, gawking at the ghosts of skyscrapers, the purple pull of the Hudson River at sunset tugging me along when Catherine finally called.

We met up at an Italian restaurant around nine, my senses flooded by her beauty and my hunger and thirst and the smells of olive oil and cheese and perfume and the density of all the city's sights and, yes, the adrenaline of my upcoming trip to Iraq.

"You're going to be famous," she said to me that night at dinner.

But more than fame, I just wanted her to love me. An expensive bottle of red wine arrived. I was going deep into debt. I was about to spend $2,000 I didn't have on a plane ticket to Kuwait. I was already in the hole for my ticket to New York and my conference fee. But there was no way I was going dutch treat with Catherine smiling at me, our feet bouncing off each other's under the table.

"How was work?" I asked.

"Let's talk about you instead," she said. "You're going to Iraq."

"I want to talk about you," I said. "I haven't seen you in like five years."

"Yeah, but I'm not going to Iraq," she said. "You're going to Iraq. Are you scared?"

I wanted to kiss her and propose marriage right then, just skip Iraq, and jump right into the next chapter of my life. My desire for her had never been stronger, which probably had something to do with my fear of death. Catherine was working for American Express. In her spare time she was trying her hand at screenwriting. She was writing funny songs about Scientology and had an idea for a sitcom, and sometimes I could just imagine us sharing a desk in a small New York apartment, swapping lines, sharing stories.

"Tell me about this pilot you're working on," I said.

"It's stupid," she said. "It involves a bunch of sassy teenage girls behaving badly, *Mean Girls* meets *Napoleon Dynamite*. It has nothing to do with Iraq."

"I went to a psychic last night," I said.

"Excuse me?"

Catherine sat up a little straighter in her chair. Despite my desire to have her do all the talking so I wouldn't seem like such a self-involved dilettante, there were a million things I wanted to tell her, and this one just came out, and for a few perilous moments, I wasn't sure why, and I felt as if I was losing her, her sudden rigid posture a reaction to my flimsy, out-of-control mind. But I couldn't stop myself. I'm a storyteller. So I told her that I'd been walking the streets when this Romanian girl with long, black, cornrowed hair had asked me if I wanted a reading. I'd never done a "reading" before. As I described to Catherine the lure of the psychic, I was afraid my wine-drunk mind was revealing too much.

But, somewhat like my country's mission in Iraq, I found my justification for my blurted-out beginning midway through, the plane built mid-flight. I told Catherine that the psychic, whose name was Ashley, fell to her knees and stared into my eyes and told me that someone was worried about my upcoming trip. Ashley told me I'd had "two pains" in the past year. She told me that I was honest but that I "go too far with the truth." She told me about someone who loved me very much, but there was jealousy. Her eyes—Ashley's—began to water. She told me I'd lost love, but that I'd find it again. I knew right there—in the middle—that that was the place to end the story. I looked Catherine in the eye. I wanted her to see that I wasn't ruined, that I was ready for love.

"How much did you pay?" she asked.

"Two bucks," I said.

"That's not bad for two bucks," she said.

I was a little glad Catherine hadn't totally bitten on my sincere eye contact, the way I'd tried to subtly bring the story of the psychic around to her. I felt half-proud for having pulled off the story and half like a fraud. We finished the bottle of wine. We talked about literature and her former boyfriend, a guy named Joe. I paid the bill. We walked the streets, laughing and talking about how we both loved pot and were both deeply skeptical of Scientology and George W. Bush. Around one in the morning we stepped into a jazz joint, a band in a corner in front of a wall with a mural of a band in a corner in front of a wall. I don't remember if we danced, but I remember feeling happy with her as we rode back to her apartment on the subway, trading presidential trivia, rat facts. James Buchanan was the only bachelor president, widowers excluded. William Howard Taft was the fattest president of them all. George H. W. Bush was once the director of the CIA. And let's not forget Tippecanoe and Tyler, too. I recited them all in order for her. We looked into each other's eyes as we geeked out on the increasingly abandoned train. She asked me if I thought I'd ever get over Karen. I didn't want to seem like George W. Bush. I didn't want to answer that question with a false sense of certitude. So I said, "I don't know."

And so I slept on her couch.

I made my way among the nine thousand writers gaggled about the New York Hilton. I followed my map through the throngs of aspiring poets and novelists, the tortoiseshell glasses and berets, the coffee sippers and phone checkers, the adjuncts and turtlenecks, the burned-out visionaries of yesterday, the tenure-grabbing, gray-haired, chapbook-wielding writers who, let's face it, might well be the Ghost of Christmas Yet to Come if I'm lucky.

"See, I don't even care about Billy Collins," said a slender woman with her arms akimbo as a Seth Rogen look-alike in an argyle sweater threw his arms to the heavens in defense of Billy Collins.

"Who are these people?" the condescending comedian in my mind asked.

"These are your people," some other voice says now.

I wanted to attend the panel about the literature of war, and I was running late. My throat was hoarse from all the talking and drinking with Catherine from the night before. I ducked into the conference room, took my seat in the back, felt instantly discouraged by all the empty seats, the unrecognizable faces with their water pitchers and microphones poised behind the cloth-draped table at the front. I considered leaving almost as soon as I'd sat down, disappointed to hear a singsong voice passionately rendering a memoirish essay about a Vietnam veteran she kinda knew.

Some people call AWP "All the Wrong People" because it's quite rare that you actually encounter the writers and or publishing personnel you really want to meet. Where was the not-yet-dead David Foster Wallace? Where was Don DeLillo? I was aching for one of these literary lions to travel deep into the war and return with a vision. Instead, I was surrounded by no-names. Who was Sandra Beasley? Who was Doug Anderson? Who the hell was Brian Turner?

Who the hell am I?

At some point, as I actually started to listen to my fellow no-name peers, I felt my resistance start to soften. Doug Anderson spoke eloquently about the marginalization of war poetry after World War I, this trend a reflection of the marginalization of the individual in a world increasingly dominated by machines, war as the embodiment of the machine, the military code essentially anti-individual. I started to take notes, perhaps a bit unsettled by the insinuations of Anderson's shaved head and silver goatee and wire-rimmed glasses. Maybe here indeed was Christmas Yet to Come. Who the hell did I think I was, judging all these aspiring writers so harshly, sitting in the back of the room with my lab notebook crafting caricatures of human beings while I myself still knew nothing of war or love or anything? I had my talking points, sure, a growing folder of documents about Al Anbar Province and the Haditha massacre, but I still didn't have body armor or official approval from CENTCOM. And my media sponsor was a literary journal that didn't yet exist, my credentialing editor an exhausted no-name just like me, just like these folks. Just before I'd left for New York, Rip had signed his name to a boilerplate letter that said that he and his nonexistent journal accepted responsibility for providing notification to next of kin in the event of the death of or injury to Matthew C. Armstrong while embedded in a hostile combat environment.

"Rumor is everything. The lie leads to the truth," one of the writers said.

Brian Turner, another war poet, began to read. He was a burly infantry leader who had seen combat in Iraq with the Third Stryker Brigade. He read from his collection *Here, Bullet.* Some sophomoric part of me wanted to mock Turner, winner of the Beatrice Hawley Award. After all, who the hell was Beatrice Hawley? There seemed to be a spinsterish woman's name sponsoring every small glossy collection that crowded the book fair downstairs. It wasn't until I arrived in New York, a month before leaving for Iraq, that I *started* to realize how small I was, how there were a million men like me in my country, shy and arrogant, sincere and cynical—thousands of confused men and women who didn't even know they were confused. I suddenly felt grateful as I listened to Turner read his poetry, poetry doing what poetry does best: it slows time. It holds the bullet midair before it enters the brain. It humbles us. It makes us listen and witness.

Brian Turner taught me a lot that day. *Sadiq* means friend in Arabic. *Ashbah* means ghost. *Jameel* means beautiful. *Shukran* means thank you. Fobbits are the names of the 99 percent in the war on terror, the folks who don't go outside the wire of the FOB, the forward operating base. Sometimes writers turn to the second person when confronting trauma in order to show how hard it is to own your emotions. Some veterans belong to PTSD writing groups, which are a significant growing demographic in the MFA communities, and perhaps the beginning of a genuine literary movement. Some veterans play video games right after a traumatic incident to replace the replay of the real trauma with a dense simulation in which they have control. Sandra Beasley looked a bit like Anne Hathaway and was actually a really good writer. I wondered if I could get her number. I wondered if I was a creep, more predator than poet. I wondered if any of these people could tell me how to find ceramic body armor. When the poetry was over, I clapped with the masses and moved with the masses toward the front of the room, hoping to steal a word or two from Turner, who was kind and passionate and patient. He gave me his autograph and email address and wrote to me on the inside of his collection: *I look forward to what your words will bring us all.*

Riding back to Catherine's on the subway, I began to read through his collection. I learned that *habib* means love. I read about the deaths of Turner's friends. I began to see another side of the war I'd been reading about in the newspapers. Here were the riots that ensued after the American invasion. Here were the animals released from the Baghdad Zoo, bears now mauling Iraqis in the streets and baboons suddenly marooned in the desert.

My god, I thought. This is horrible and beautiful. I have no idea what I'm doing. There's no way I'm turning back. As I stood against a pole waiting to transfer to another train, I felt alive and focused, my mission clear: I needed to learn how to see again, like Turner, like a poet. I needed to write down everything I saw in Iraq, talk to every man and woman I could meet. I felt like I'd been waiting my entire life for the chance to see what my country was all about, and I was tired of being cynical and dismissive, pretending like I could see without the help of others, my judgmental juvenile caricature-crazy tendencies my greatest liability as a writer. If I was going to truly see the holy lands, Babylon, the Garden of Eden—Iraq—I needed to become more *eye*, less *I*.

I needed to lose myself.

I felt a swat on my arm, fell out of my mind. I wheeled around and found another guy with a shaved head and a goatee. He wore a blue scarf and a black leather jacket.

"Mike?" he said.

"No," I said.

The stranger apologized, threw his hands up in a gesture of arrest. I smiled. Sometimes it feels good to be nobody, to know that you can blend into a landscape with your standard white features and your hairless head, your little trimmed goatee, your stock military physique. Maybe this—

this blending in—is what the writer truly needs. I heard the roar of my train and stepped toward the tracks, watched the slots of splotchy faces roll into the station, felt the warmth of all those surging bodies touching and dodging me, everybody doing the best they could not to stare at each other once we were all seated and the train started to move into the dark tunnels of the underground.

I was told in mid-February by Specialist James T. Deady that my request to embed was still pending and to hold off on purchasing my ticket. At the end of every email I received from Deady was the following quote from the movie *Office Space*: "Human beings were not meant to sit in little cubicles staring at computer screens all day, filling out useless forms and listening to eight different bosses drone on about mission statements." Like me, this man wanted out of his cubicle, but he was in the war—and was *still* feeling the strain, the cage.

This was a fobbit.

I went over my journalist requirements, tried to check all my boxes in my attempt to get out of my box. I still couldn't find my required class 4 body armor. In addition to requiring purchase of a vest and a helmet, the military also wanted evidence of my credibility as a writer. I sent them digital copies of several poems I'd written, including one about the Grateful Dead. This was my evidence of my seriousness as a journalist: a brief piece of doggerel about the Dead. I felt like I was screwed.

Yet Public Affairs Officer Reynolds emailed that there were no loaners on the body armor front. I had to provide my own. I drove around town in limbo, not wanting to spend money on body armor if I didn't have a plane ticket, and I didn't want to buy a ticket if I didn't have clearance to embed, and I was sure that after reading my poems on the Grateful Dead the military was going to laugh in my face. My father was right. The *Winchester Star* was right. What the hell was I doing? I wasn't a journalist. I didn't know a thing about cultivating sources. I didn't even like the way most journalists wrote except for guys like Hunter S. Thompson. If anybody could appreciate this goose chase, this idiot with a shaved head trying to con his way onto the front lines of the war on terror, it was Hunter S. Thompson.

"Journalism," Thompson wrote in *Fear and Loathing in Las Vegas*, "is not a profession or a trade. It is a cheap catch-all for fuckoffs and misfits—a false doorway to the backside of life, a filthy piss-ridden little hole nailed off by the building inspector, but just deep enough for a wino to curl up from the sidewalk and masturbate like a chimp in a zoo-cage."

The closer I got to Iraq, the more I admired those chimps, the harried men and women who tramped all over the globe in search of stories, compelled by a usefully naive search for the "backside of life," the truth. Yes, there was a dark, innocent thrill in walking into a gun store in late February and searching for body armor, feeling the admiration of rednecks who wished they could see the holy lands blown to smithereens, men who wondered out loud why we hadn't just nuked the whole goddamned place into one big sheet of fucking glass. But whether they envied or admired me or despised me, those gun-store clerks refused to sell me body armor. They all kept referring to some burglar from California who'd evaded the cops far longer than he should've by virtue of his vest, taking a few of the dicks with him before finally getting gunned down in the streets.

"There's a YouTube video of it somewhere," one of them said.

Running out of options, starting to feel desperate, like this one little unchecked box might keep me out of Iraq, I drove to the sheriff's office in downtown Greensboro. Sheriff B. J. Barnes was friendly to me. He didn't make me wait. I'd met him ten years before, when I was writing a story about a man in jail. Barnes had allowed me to tour the downtown lockup, to smell the smells and hear the cries. When I asked if I could borrow a bulletproof vest for my trip to Iraq, this man who could pass for the lovechild of Dick Cheney and Joe Don Baker asked who I was writing for.

"*Convergence Quarterly.*"

"Who?"

"We're an interdisciplinary journal."

"A what?"

"We're new," I said. "And we're kinda low on funds."

He shook his head and smiled. He laughed. He said he wished he could help me but couldn't risk the responsibility of something happening. I said I'd heard that one before. He showed me the door and patted me on the back. He wished me luck.

But I was worried. Spring break was close. As a college instructor, the spring holiday was my only window of time to see the war. I had to get my paperwork approved within the next few days if I wanted a plane ticket to Kuwait that wouldn't forever enslave me to my creditors. Money was a real issue. In addition to the $2,000 I'd have to spend on a ticket if I were lucky enough to get approved, the body armor, if I could find some, would cost me at least $400 to $500, maybe three times that much if I wanted SEAL-grade ceramic, and, on top of all this, now that the *Winchester Star* had pulled out, thanks to my father, there was no guarantee that anyone would buy my stories once I returned. More to the point, there was no guarantee I'd even return, and this, more than anything, helped to minimize the anxiety about money.

But the man about to meet his maker says, "Who cares about 20 percent interest? Just put it on my card."

Then, sure enough, I got a call from Iraq. Diet had just had word from Reynolds that a Colonel Connors had been reviewing my application in CENTCOM and that, as luck would have it, Colonel Connors was a James Wood Colonel, James Wood being the Winchester, Virginia, high school Diet and I attended for two years before transferring to the brand-new Sherando High School, where we became Warriors.

"Apparently," Diet said, "Connors thinks you can't be all bad if you're a Colonel. So you're in, Eat Boy. Get your fucking ticket."

I went for a jubilant delusional sunset run. The next day I stormed into the office and found Rip hunched over papers in his cubicle. "CQ is a go." He wheeled around in his chair and shook my hand and told me not to die.

I took his accreditation letter to a Kinko's shop and got it laminated, believing this is what journalists did. I wanted my official documents in a manila folder. I wanted them laminated. On February 28, at 7:35 p.m., I was leaving for Kuwait, and from Kuwait I would travel to Baghdad, and from Baghdad I would make my way via chopper or convoy to one of the most dangerous cities in the world—Haditha, site of the Haditha massacre.

I was two weeks away. I bought a digital recorder. I bought a CD and crib sheet for basic Iraqi Arabic called *Accent on Iraq*. I found a bulletproof helmet at an army navy surplus store. I read wildly about everything Iraqi I could get my hands on. I read about scorpions and cobras and camel spiders, death stalkers. I read about leishmaniasis. I read about the differences between Sunnis and Shiites and Sufis. I read every account I could find on the Haditha massacre.

And then, on February 28, after that moment when Karen confessed she still loved me and after I'd finally scored some shitty, low-grade body armor at Southern Firearms, I drove to downtown Greensboro past the Woolworth's storefront where the civil rights sit-in movement began, still oblivious to the fact that the peaceful protesters from that historic lunch counter shared an alma mater with the not-so-peaceful mastermind of 9/11.

That night of the twenty-eighth, Dr. Graves, the great evolutionary biologist and my boss at North Carolina A&T—the best boss I've ever had—took me and several of my close friends out for a farewell dinner at Natty Greene's, a Greensboro pub named after the city's namesake, the young, debt-ridden Revolutionary War hero who fought valiantly against Cornwallis. Nathanael Greene was one of those rare figures in military history who was famous for having pulled off a strategic retreat, saving the lives of thousands of American soldiers, his defeat a victory in the eyes of history.

"Do you guys want a beer?" the waitress asked.

"He's going to Iraq," my friend Jenny said.

"What?!" the waitress exclaimed with a big wide smile, suggesting men weren't the only ones who thought of war as more than just misery and death.

At dinner that night were Jenny Noller, J. T. Hill, Dr. Graves, and yours truly. Jenny and J.T. had been members of my fiction workshop at UNCG, two of my closest friends. Jenny, a beautiful Georgia blonde who understood my passion for writing, had haunted my relationship with Karen, often filling her—Karen—with a dread that I would leave her for a writer one day, maybe Jenny herself. As it turned out, I left Karen not for a writer but to some extent for writing itself—the monastic solitude to do what I felt I needed to do. On my way out the door, J.T., an extremely funny and talented blind writer from West Virginia, handed me a note and told me not to open it until I was up in the air. Because he was blind, J.T. rarely looked you in the eye, but I could see he was crying. We'd been through a lot together. I'd recently driven down to Nashville to pack him up and drive him back to Greensboro after his divorce from an ex-Mormon poet. For a moment, in 2005, we'd both been happily engaged writers who felt the world was our oyster. Things had changed, but I was glad he was back in town and still writing, and I couldn't believe he was crying. I gave him a hug, felt some tears of my own. I gave Jenny a hug, took heart from Dr. Graves's big thwack on my back, and then drove down the road toward Piedmont Triad International Airport.

I took a connector to Dulles, sat across the aisle from a white North Carolina A&T student, a striking brunette named Brittney who was sucking on a smoothie from Dunkin' Donuts and who told me she was on her way to Kansas for spring break and wondered what classes I taught, saying she'd love to take me. She reached across the aisle and put the long press-on nail of her forefinger on top of my hand as she started to tell me her dream, her goal of one day opening up a gas station in California, one of these one-stop shopping hubs you increasingly see on the roadsides of our country, except her mini-mart would not only have organic groceries and healthy sandwiches and magazines and beer and candy and clothing but also a clinic where you could get a colonic in the rear, no pun intended.

"People in California love colonics," she said.

Walking through the Dulles terminal past newsstands and fast food restaurants, I imagined clients in the back getting powerful jet streams of saltwater gunned up their asses. I liked the idea and the ghost of the feeling of Brittney's press-on nail atop my hand. I felt good. My boxes were checked. I had my body armor and my laminated letter of sponsorship. I sat down in front of the gate for my flight to Kuwait, suddenly surrounded by real American soldiers. I pulled out my manila folder and started to read about the Al Anbar Awakening, but suddenly I couldn't stop hearing the echo of Karen's words:

"I love you."

Light and loose turned to tight and scared. I stared at my cell phone, the long hallway of that Dulles terminal suddenly haunting, the embodiment of *terminal*, the end of the line, the choice of death over love, my mind trapped in that binary box. I felt like a zombie as I followed the soldiers onto the plane. I was at least a little relieved to see big seats and wide aisles. I sat next to a man named Ryan Brazile, who turned out to be a Cheyenne Indian from the Blackfeet Reservation in Montana. I told him my name and saw his eyes open to the utterance of "Armstrong." I began to relax as he told me stories. He said that the Blackfeet Reservation was next door to the site of the Battle of Little Bighorn, where George Armstrong Custer and his Seventh Cavalry had been routed by the Cheyenne.

"My brother's now a member of the Seventh Cavalry," he said.

"That's some irony," I said.

"Yeah," he said.

I looked down at the dark leathery crawl of the Atlantic Ocean at night, looked around at the faces in the cabin, saw two large black women chatting amicably under their reading lights, wondered how they, too, had come to see the Global War on Terror as their own. I turned on my light and read through articles about the recent assassinations of sheikhs in Al Anbar Province, Al Qaeda apparently taking out everyone they could who was cooperating with the United States.

I started to feel uneasy as I read further. Attacks on Sunnis had doubled over the last year. Americans were handing out cash to sheikhs and incorporating new technology to minimize casualties, slowly integrating "Reaper" drones and replacing Humvees with MRAPs, or mine resistant ambush protection vehicles, which had stronger reinforced floorboards than the Humvees. I looked down at my legs. I thought about the clipping my mother had sent me, the story about David Bloom, an embedded reporter who'd sat still for too long in the tank he'd been traveling in and died of a deep vein thrombosis. So, in the name of saving my legs, I took a walk up the aisle, did a little yoga. I watched a cartoon jet crawl across a map on the screen at the front of the plane, dozed off for a while, and awoke to see thin desert clouds, sprawling sand flats, oily coils of inland water, the northwest coast of the Persian Gulf.

I opened up the note from J.T. It said: "Chad Starr prays for your safe return."

Chad Starr was the name of a character in a novel J.T. was working on, a child actor who was a mock tribute to the evangelical actor Kirk Cameron. I found J.T.'s note touching, his emotions always coded in pop culture references and nervous jokes. Unlike every other writer I called a friend, J. T. Hill knew for a fact that he was blind.

Ryan Brazile woke up and asked me where I was headed. I told him I was embedding with SEALs in Haditha. He nodded, gave me his email address, told me he'd been eating at the DFAC in Mosul on the day of the famous pre-Christmas bombing by Abu Omar the year before. I nodded. But the truth was, I knew nothing about Abu Omar. I didn't even know the name of the guy who'd started the war.

We shook hands and walked off the plane. I heard the hawky, phlegmy sound of Arabic voices up ahead and over the public address system. I felt an immediate sense of vigilance, strangeness, danger. We were now in Kuwait, my first time ever in the Middle East. I saw the dots and swirls of Arabic all over the airport signs, clueless looking Americans in tropical shirts looking down in consternation at their serviceless cell phones, dreadlocked Kuwaitis with serious bling looking paranoid, constantly looking over their shoulders, jazzy horns playing softly over the airport sound system, curry and perfume in the air, beads in the hands of several sheikhish men, red-and-white tea cloth headwraps galore, some women with only a thread of skin revealed, others with tall boots and bursting busts, their headwear seeming nothing more than a token nod to Islam.

I found the Starbucks where I was supposed to meet my military contact. I wondered if I should walk inside or stay out in the open.

"You over here contracting?" I heard a man with a hard-shelled briefcase ask another. The other guy, who was sipping a coffee and wearing a white shirt and a dark suit with no tie, answered without saying a word. Here was one thing I did know and was very interested in: the contractor was playing an increasingly large role in this war. I wanted to understand the role of corporate America in the Global War on Terror, the fact that more than 50 percent of the personnel in Iraq could be categorized as corporate, profit-driven, professional, not accountable to the same standards as our troops, not accountable to voters. In other words, mercenaries. Were the guys from Blackwater and Halliburton the picture of twenty-first-century evil? To what degree did the corporatization of war alter the American and Iraqi attitude toward Operation Iraqi Freedom? To what degree did it alter the idea of America itself? Everywhere I went in my country, I had the sense that people truly didn't care about the war, and who could blame them? Maybe it wasn't *our* war. Maybe all the atrocities belonged to Dick Cheney and Erik Prince, the founder of Blackwater. Without a draft, our wars—our troops—didn't belong to us anymore, not in the way they had in the past. During the 1991 Gulf War, contractor presence was less than 10 percent, but now, with the majority of participants corporate, it was hard to deny the motive behind our presence in an oil-rich country that had had no hand in the attacks of 9/11. On my return trip from Iraq I would meet a contractor who would change my life, a man whose revelation would forever change the way I saw my generation's war.

But a fortnight before that, I met Andrew, my military handler, and then the two staffers from the *Atlanta Journal and Constitution*, Moni and Curtis. On the way to the Ali Al Salem base in Kuwait, Moni peppered me with questions while Curtis, her photographer, sat quietly against the window of our van. I saw a sign for a Kentucky Fried Chicken, large tracts of fence-protected sand providing more and more of the scene as we approached the base. Moni, it turned out, was also interested in the contractor angle, but her engagement with the issue was much more nuanced than mine. Moni looked about forty, a light floss of gray in her thick dark hair. She wore a wedding ring, a pair of glasses perched atop her head.

"Do you know what a 3PN is?"

This was like the fiftieth term she'd mentioned that I didn't understand. There was no bluffing this woman, no way she was going to see me as her equal, so it was best to just start being honest and humble. It's not exactly accurate to say I "played the fool" with Moni. The fact was, I *was* the fool. I told her I'd never heard the term "3PN" and knew next to nothing about this whole process and that I'd be deeply indebted to her if she'd just tell me everything she knew. She greeted my confession with raised eyebrows and an ovular tautening of her lips.

She explained that 3PN was a name for third-party nationals, the invisible people I was about to see all over the base: the Eritrean ID checkers, the Pakistani and Indonesian cooks, the Filipino garbage collectors—in other words, the people who weren't white, the dark people, the workers. These jobs used to go to American soldiers, but our government had outsourced them to the wage slaves of third-world countries, and because these workers were represented by third-party contractors, Americans had no responsibility for their conditions or the abuse they might endure. It was all about money and avoiding accountability.

"What about them?" my father had asked.

Well, when I arrived at the base DFAC for my first military breakfast, there they were with their rubber gloves and dark faces and impossible smiles. Over and over, this was one of the profound lessons of my journey. No matter how bad the conditions or how heinous the historical context, I kept seeing smiles, the faces of people full of goodwill or faking goodwill, and because I didn't know how to translate such smiles, I just did what felt natural: when the smiling Indonesian man with bright white teeth spooned curried chicken onto my paper plate and said "good morning," I said "good morning" and smiled back. I sat down at a table by myself and wrote in my journal while a war movie played on a big-screen TV.

I took note of how the room seemed under the spell of the screen and the white male hero saving the day in the standard two-hour cinematic time frame. But I also joined the spell. I said a prayer before I ate. I prayed, as I often did, for my mother's survival but now also for my own.

I'd made it to Kuwait, the Ali Al Salem air base. I'd be leaving in less than forty-eight hours for Baghdad. I ate my cubes of curried chicken and big heaping mounds of salad. I wolfed down mac and cheese, helped myself to a hamburger and freedom fries and an ice cream sandwich. I put my tray on a conveyor belt and tried to see the scene behind the flopping plastic cloths that protected the diners from the workers, the steam-shrouded dark skin and gloved hands of workers who knew nothing of dental plans.

After that dinner for breakfast, I walked across the morning sand through the sprawl of the camp, full of the faces of the workers. I stared out on the vast bivouac, the endless rows of tents for soldiers and contractors, spies and cooks, men and women from all over the world here in Kuwait looking for a piece of the wartime pie. Stadium-style lights towered over the sunrise compound. Dark birds I'd never seen before fought over crusts of bread in the sand, conducting what looked like a rugby match as they clustered and surged around the scrap.

I wished I was sharing a tent with Moni and Curtis. Instead, as I ducked beneath the flaps of my canvas hut in the middle of this anonymous Hooverville of wartime workers, I realized I was sleeping among strangers, the 3PNs. I took off my shoes. I pulled out an old throwaway bedsheet from my duffel bag, a floral liner I'd taken from the deep recesses of the upstairs linen closet when I'd been home for Christmas, a nostalgic nod to the bed of my boyhood. It felt good to feel the cool cotton and smell the soapy hints of home. From my top bunk I looked through squinted eyelids at the dark faces of the other men in my tent, all of us brought together by the dream of the war in Iraq.

# 9. MARCH 2008

## IRAQ AND KUWAIT

Chuck Norris once walked down
a street with a raging erection.
There were no survivors.
—GRAFFITI FROM THE WAR

I met another woman on the morning I flew out of Haditha. I'd awak-
ened early, yet on less than three hours' sleep I felt more alive than I had
in years. The dry desert wind washed over me as I closed my eyes to the
morning sun, wishing to imprint this memory for a lifetime: "This is Iraq.
This is Iraq." I looked up at the dam, the workers like figurines moving
through a concrete hive, a child's diorama. I walked alone for a while,
studying the base—Nickel Base—one more time. I thought about the
captain and the mayor and Diet and the laughter we'd found on the edge
of violence, and I thought about the burn pits, the strange growth on the
sheikh's leg. I thought about the stories I could tell and the ones I couldn't.

I was about to catch a chopper back to Baghdad. They were calling for
sandstorms the next day, so I needed to be out on that morning flight.
Then, as I started toward the dam, I met a woman with curly black hair
and a crooked smile, and that morning she was tending a garden with
a bucket sprinkler. I approached her and looked down at parsley and
sprouting tomato plants and radishes.

Her name was Lucy. She wore a black wool toboggan on her head and
a black fleece over her green fatigues. She was a missionary, back in Iraq
to help her people. We talked about her garden and the dogs she was

feeding before she told me her story. Lucy had grown up on the outskirts of Baghdad, lost a brother in Iraq's war with Iran, and left the country in 1984 when Iraq and the United States were working not so secretly together to overthrow Iran's leader, Ayatollah Khomeini. Lucy was living in St. Louis when Operation Iraqi Freedom began. I stood with her that March morning, five years after the invasion, looking down at the little sprigs of herbs and vegetables she had planted. There were two stray mutts loyally threading through her legs.

"It is hopeless," she said. "You can listen to what they say all day, but when you replace one tribe with another tribe you will still have tribalism, and that is the tragedy of Iraq, and that will continue to be the tragedy of Iraq and the world. There is no structural change here. There is no structural change anywhere."

Tribes, corporations, parties—our founding fathers had used the term "factions" to describe the greatest of all dangers to democracy, but maybe "tribes" cuts more to the chase. There's a primitive quality to that word that advertising experts and public relations gurus love to capitalize on. Find your tribe, they say. Find your niche and capitalize. Divide and conquer. Double down on the base. Don't you dare try to advance that notion that we're all connected, all one. Iraq over here. Iran over there. Fox over here. CNN over there. SEALs on one side of the river, contractors on the other—marines like the godhead bridging the gap, looking down from the dam on the river that divides the American military tribe.

But of course I wasn't seeing any of that godhead business by the garden. There was no final foreboding epiphany about the Haditha dam as some great literary embodiment of the dammed-up ancient rivers that connect us all. No, in the moment I was just making small talk, killing time before my chopper arrived. Lucy told me she had family in Rome and the Netherlands, folks all over the world. When she told me she prayed in the chapel inside the dam every morning, I experienced a little snap, crackle, and pop of awareness that the dam was more complicated than I imagined—it was the first time that it even occurred to me that there might be something other than military-industrial activities taking place inside that architectural monstrosity, but I didn't press. Lucy told me that prayer, gardening, and studying architecture helped her pass her time in Iraq, that she tried to avoid TV.

"The screen is like a drug," she said.

Lucy's big goal was soliciting donations for hospitals and schools, helping her people to rebuild their country. I began to admire her tremendously, which is to say, I started to feel like I needed more time in Iraq, more than just this spring fortnight, this tightly plotted glimpse. As I spoke to Lucy and stroked the ears of the dogs, I knew it was time to go, but I wanted to stay. I didn't know exactly what I needed to look for, but I could feel the mysteries of Haditha everywhere. I looked over her shoulder, saw once again the red, spray-painted letters "KBR" on the wall in front of the shacks across the river. I was about to leave this camp on the banks of the Euphrates. I only had a few minutes, not enough time for a swim. I hadn't gotten one word out of those KBR employees whose lives didn't count in the casualty tallies, those corporate jack-of-all-trades who lived so quietly over there, burning the garbage and who knew what else. Lucy kept talking. I didn't want her to stop. She said that the life of an architect focuses "on structure." In Iraq, however, she felt herself to be in the opposite position. She was now a missionary, no longer concerned with the big picture, now a slave to the detail known as the human being.

I watched a dog take a shit on her garden, saw her face crease with a smile I will never forget. I thought this was it, the end of the story, the dog taking a shit on the soil being a crass but not an entirely worthless metaphor. Maybe scatology offers us some of our most fruitful lenses for framing the stories of this particular war.

I walked back to Diet's room to give him a hug. He gave me a brass commemorative coin, an eagle with a trident and a gun on one side, a fish and a beret and the words "SEAL Team One" on the other. He gave me a flag to give to my father. I felt close to tears as I stood at the top of the dam against the wind of the chopper's rotors and I took a last look at the fertile curves of the Euphrates River, the palm trees that thinned into elephant grass and then sand—desert as far as you could see.

I fastened my chinstrap. I put my earplugs in and ducked my head. With Reynolds and a random, bald, middle-aged contractor by my side, I flew back to Al Asad, and from Al Asad I took a night chopper back to Baghdad, and at one point I think we were fired on, but maybe it was nothing more than a tracer trailing across the sky. No one leaned over to tell me what I had seen, and because I was always embarrassed by how little I knew, I never took the time to ask the tense clutch of men in the cabin of that chopper, "WHAT THE HELL WAS THAT?"

I tell of this moment aware that the media is now being referred to as "the enemy of the people" by President Trump and that NBC newscaster Brian Williams lost his job for lying about getting shot at while in Iraq. I understand that temptation to lie, to feather fiction into fact. I know why false reporting happens. Fear is a strange fountain. The truth is slippery. But the truth is, I don't know what happened. The moment passed. I caught my breath, once again looked down on the sapphire lights of Baghdad's suburban neighborhoods. At three in the morning, nearly delirious with exhaustion, I strapped into a C-130 Hercules and flew back to Kuwait, 3,975 American soldiers dead as of that morning, the number of dead Iraqis perhaps the darkest mystery of my generation.

After flying back into Kuwait from Baghdad, I returned to the plentiful buffets of the Ali Al Salem Air Base dining facility, always referred to as the DFAC (DEE-fack). I ate a meal of Jell-O, egg rolls, rotisserie chicken, and rice and beans. I eavesdropped on the soldiers and the contracted Pakistani cooks mumbling in their paper crowns, war movies always playing on the screens on the walls. I thought my work was done. I felt more than lucky to be alive.

What I mean by saying that I felt "more than lucky" is that I somehow felt my life and health to be evidence of a happy ending on the way for our soldiers and the people of Iraq. I had no idea, as I feasted in that buffet and took notes for my stories, that I had stumbled upon one of the great public health crises of our time. I did not know that countless veterans would come forward with a wide array of mysterious ailments that would point to burn pit symptoms as the Agent Orange or the Gulf War syndrome of our time. I had no idea that ten years after my embed, Republicans and Democrats would actually come together to propose and pass legislation to fund the treatment of American veterans exposed to burn pits and, in so doing, entirely ignore the Iraqis who still lived on the soil and by the rivers that were still polluted with the burn pit toxins. No, because I was safe and sound, I believed the same could be said for the country of Iraq.

Sitting in that DFAC, drinking my suicide punch (i.e., a little squirt of every soda), I began to fill my notebooks with the stories I had gathered. I had nearly a hundred pages of notes from interviews with Iraqi soldiers, police chiefs, and politicians, and I had not forgotten Sheikh D'han Hussein D'meithan or his son. I looked at the pictures I had taken of the cancerous lesions on the sheikh's leg. I wanted to tell the readers of the *Winchester Star* about his son's cancer treatments and how his family had been bankrupted. But the story was not yet clear to me. Rami had been the first person to show me a burn pit. I was the only journalist to document the Haditha burn pit, as far as I know, but not only did I not know that then, I also had no clue as to just how complicated those unregulated fires were and how they might be connected to other stories.

What I thought would be important and digestible for my readers was a clear before-and-after narrative focused on Haditha, its citizens, and our hometown hero, Diet, the Navy SEAL whom I had known in high school. The story would go something like this: In 2005 a marine platoon was traveling in a convoy in Haditha. A bomb went off, and the Third Battalion, First Regiment, descended into a chaos that gave most American readers their first glimpse of Haditha: the Haditha massacre. But things were getting better, right? This was just the "before." As I sat in the Ali Al Salem DFAC, I still thought it was possible that Hadithans might receive justice for the Haditha massacre, the murder of twenty-four of their people. I didn't know that America would wait until after the Iraq War was over (will it ever be over?) to dismiss all serious charges against the marines and that James Mattis, who served two years as secretary of defense, would be one of the officers responsible for clearing our troops of responsibility.

However, the injustice had not yet been done. The Hadithans had not yet been insulted by our disregard for that incident or the pollution of their water and soil via the burn pits. With such verdicts still up in the air and my young, optimistic disposition presiding, I decided to focus my stories on the simple statistics of violence and the key police officials on both sides who seemed to be fundamentally responsible for the reduction of attacks in Haditha and its surrounding hamlets. I told the story of Diet, the hometown hero, and how Captain Al'a, a former thief and scavenger who wore a feathered mullet, had seen several members of his family beheaded but was now the charismatic leader of the Iraqi SWAT team Diet's men had trained.

I was proud of myself as I began to scribble together my profile of this Iraqi cop with his mullet and his checkered history. I was almost giddy with gratitude, a sense of my own good fortune. My father was terrified that his son would be kidnapped and beheaded in Iraq and that he would thus lose his father, his wife, and his son in the same year, but I was now safe and I couldn't wait to show my father the evidence that all was well. I wolfed down my food and crafted a first draft of a story about a city that had once been riddled with problems but, thanks to a man with a mullet and his American mentors, was now back on track.

I walked out of the DFAC and looked up at the stars over the base. The air was cool and dry. I noticed Australian soldiers, with their mitochondrial-patterned camo, drinking sodas on a set of bleachers. I tacked to the latrines, where I would notice nothing suspicious in my bowel movement. Forty-eight hours later I would suffer a long spell of buttery diarrhea, and for several days after I was back in my office as an English teacher, I noticed that I was forgetting the names of my students at North Carolina A&T, the historically black college that educated the mastermind of 9/11 back in the 1980s. But just as the college liked to forget the tenure of Khalid Sheikh Mohammed, I was able to forget my forgetting and my diarrhea and the burn pits for years.

Yes, I had happy stories to tell and I aimed to tell them. I stepped into my tent and rested my notebook on the top bunk where I'd stretched my childhood bedsheet over a cheap, thin mattress. I did not want to indict my country for its behavior in Iraq. I wanted to give the best spin I could give. I wanted to share what good news I could find, and I wanted to go to sleep atop that cool familiar sheet, that floral liner. But then a man walked into that tent, and my life has never been the same since.

Just before midnight, on March 11, 2008, that man began unpacking his bags on the bunk next to mine. He looked like a gray-haired Philip Seymour Hoffman on steroids, or so I wrote in my notebook.

"You hungry?" I asked the man.

"Starved," he said.

I let him know that the DFAC was still open. He asked me where I'd been. When I told him Haditha, he said, "They show you what they found at the base of the dam?"

Not wanting to sound as ignorant as I suddenly felt, I told the man a bit about what Diet and his men had shown me: an Iraqi SWAT team captained by a charismatic thief with a mullet, a bombed-out girls' school, and a bankrupted sheikh whose son had cancer. I told him we'd hunted for Al Qaeda in the Al Jazira desert, which was sprawled out behind the Haditha dam and Lake Qadisiyah, the reservoir that fed into the Euphrates through the dam. I used the proper names as best as I could. I told the man I saw the dam every day, camped as I was on the east side of the Euphrates. But I also admitted that I never spent more than a half hour inside of it, because the dam wasn't the domain of the SEALs and the Joint Special Operations Force with whom I'd embedded. The marines held the dam. When I told the man as much, he told me that was a real shame.

"'Cuz inside that dam's the story of the war. If you've got contacts, call them up. See what they can tell you. But I was there the night EOD [Explosive Ordnance Disposal] made the discovery," he told me. "Chemical Ali's stash pile."

If this were a movie, here would be the moment the music stopped. Or started. It took me more than a second to register the weight of the contractor's disclosure. During the vast bulk of my time in Iraq I had been accompanied by Reynolds, the mustachioed public affairs officer who was very good about making sure I was never alone. The effect a constant chaperone has on the information an embedded journalist receives cannot be underestimated, but you can forget that effect while you're there, just like after a while you can forget you're wearing glasses or contact lenses.

That night in that tent in Kuwait was one of the only moments of my tour in which I was entirely unsupervised.

When I said to the contractor "you gotta be kidding me," he shook his head and smiled ruefully. We began to talk, to have an unmonitored conversation. He told me he came from Mississippi. I told him I came from North Carolina. I asked question after question, found out as much as I could about this man who had walked into my tent and about this weapons discovery at the Haditha dam.

Here's a sample of my scribbles from my notebook:

*Mr. X of Haditha.*
*Dam lore.*
*Training in Miss.*
*Former KBR. Now DynCorps MRAP rep. @ Dam in July/August '07.*
*Ali's chemical weapons.*

I'll never forget how his face grew red and the way he seemed to be playing bloody knuckles with himself as he started to remember his time in Haditha. He told me that in July 2007 he'd been driving through Al Anbar Province to deliver fuel to bases. He returned to the Haditha dam one night in the midst of an incident with a considerable amount of excitement. He, along with quite a few others, witnessed a massive EOD (Explosive Ordnance Disposal detachment) discovery of secret weapons, and thus he had been compelled to sign a confidentiality agreement. He claimed that all EOD personnel present that night had been retired on the spot. WMDs had been found at the base of the Haditha dam, sarin and cyclosarin, massive quantities of nerve gas—the same stuff we're still finding all over Iraq's next-door neighbor, Syria—and god how our amnesia serves us well. God how we love to pretend that none of it is connected.

"I'll be right back," I said to him that night.

I ran over to the recreation tent to send an email to Diet. I felt like this was a time-sensitive story. Chemical Ali, the mastermind of Iraq's chemical weapons program, was still alive in March 2008, but like Saddam Hussein, he had been sentenced to death—censorship in the Global War on Terror implemented through executions, assassinations, and the silences we can maintain through our secret prisons.

"He's playing you," Diet wrote, before telling me not to go looking for some "big story."

But I didn't go looking. I'd just started a conversation about food in the middle of the night with a stranger who, for whatever reason, was now breaking his confidentiality agreement about a classified discovery of WMDs. The guy couldn't stop talking.

I immediately consulted J. Warren Frazier, my agent, and asked for advice, feeling it was important to document my conversation with this contractor in as many ways as I could by creating a paper trail. I sought out sources from EOD. I returned to my tent and confronted the contractor with my friend's claim that he—the contractor—was "playing" me.

"When did your friend's platoon arrive in Haditha?" the contractor asked.

Diet had arrived in Haditha in October 2007. Thus, he and his men wouldn't necessarily have been privy to intelligence about a weapons discovery at the dam in July or August. But let's allow for a moment that Diet was right and the contractor was indeed playing me. I certainly took that possibility seriously. I paced around the recreation tent, watched soldiers play Ping-Pong, aware of the metaphor. What if I *was* being played? What if this guy wasn't a whistle-blower but instead a spook—a spy? Well, what that possibility seemed to suggest to me was a deliberate campaign of fake news, misinformation—propaganda—a possibility that was nearly as interesting as a genuine revelation of WMDs. Either scenario pointed to an America that had lost its way, its will to confront the truth.

I told the contractor that if his information was accurate, Bush's war was justified, so why wasn't the administration capitalizing on this game-changing story? I stood against my bunk bed as dark-skinned workers slept in the beds across the aisle and a powerful KBR fan filled our quarters with refrigerated air. The contractor told me that he and his brother had worked for KBR for a couple of years before he'd taken his current assignment with DynCorps. His duty in Iraq now, in March 2008, was to demonstrate to the troops how to use the new MRAPs, the mine-resistant ambush protection vehicles that were being distributed to platoons thanks, strangely enough, to the marine whistle-blower, Franz Gayl, the soldier-engineer who had leaked government documents about the insufficient armor of the Humvee. Gayl had been furious at the Bush administration for continuing to permit the unnecessary deaths of American soldiers. Gayl had tried to go up the chain of command, but his complaints about

Humvee casualties had been ignored, so Gayl broke the law in the name of a higher law. He broke his contract.

My contractor source told me he was getting sick of KBR in 2007, that same subsidiary of Halliburton that operated the burn pits I had sniffed. And photographed. He told me he used to make $3,800 a month, but now they were giving his job to "foreigners" for $600 a month. The contractor's justification for blowing the whistle, for violating the confidentiality agreement, was simple: KBR didn't hold up their end of the bargain. They didn't care about their people, the Americans. They were derelict in their duty, negligent in providing security for their employees. He and his brother were constantly shot at as they drove their nighttime fuel convoys across the roads of Iraq. He said that people like me, the media, were also to blame for this injustice insofar as it was the corporation's fear of the media that made them so cowardly, so unwilling to protect their workers. He said he'd often arrive at the dam furious, his trailer riddled with holes.

I could imagine his anger and fear, a terrified man in a foreign country screaming into a CB radio as his truck's getting rocked with fire. I could imagine the exasperated conversations he must have had with his brother in their camp along the Euphrates, their doubts about the courage and integrity of their employers and their country perhaps a more precise mirror of the cloudy suspicions other Americans expressed about Dick Cheney and his former company. What do you do if you're in the contractor's shoes? What do you do about such complaints—such rage—other than scrawl perversions and screeds on the walls of the very latrines you are paid to both provide and clean?

"Why classify evidence that could justify the war?" I asked.

"One or two reasons," the contractor told me. "They might still release it, might use it for political advantage before the election. But more likely, they won't. Because the weapons they found are like *all* the weapons they've found in this war. They've got our serial numbers all over 'em, bud. That's what they're afraid of."

That bit about the serial numbers hit me hard. If this were true, this was indeed "the story of the war," the secret that shattered the tribal binary of WMDs or no WMDs, myth of the Left versus myth of the Right. The contractor arched his eyebrows and squinted, that pained, ruddy crinkle a look I will never forget.

I needed air, so I left the tent and looked out on the hundreds of other windowless tan tents and canvas roofs arrayed under the stadium lights of Ali Al Salem Air Base. I took my notebook to the latrine, where I could sit on the can and write with a degree of privacy. I took note of the graffiti on the wall, felt like everything was coming together and falling apart:

KBR: *Keep Bush Rich*

*Hey Army, Marines, Air Force, Navy, Keep the war going so I can keep making 150,000 a year tax free while you dumb ass military idiots talk shit about each other on the bathroom walls making 30–50 a year!! I love this country. Signed, A Military Contractor.*

I returned to the tent, where I spent my last night in Kuwait tossing and turning atop that floral childhood sheet, surrounded by sleeping contractors. Some part of the anger from that man from Mississippi had gotten into me, and I didn't know what to do with his story. I thought about the burn pits and the WMDs disclosure, the way it shattered the conventional partisan divide, liberals saying there were no WMDs, conservatives saying yes there were. This was infuriating to me. Just as in the climate change debate, both sides knew the truth, but someone was invested in the truth staying concealed. If this working-class figure was telling me the truth, then what about his story threatened the folks above his pay grade? Why was this story not getting out? Iraq did have WMDs and they—these weapons, this stamp of evil—had a source. And that source was us, the only country to ever actually use nuclear weapons on other people. Dear god. I could feel how this story tied me back to my grandfather and his role in the Manhattan Project, but I also wondered if Diet was right—if I was being played. But if that was true, the plot to conceal—to scramble the public with misinformation—was even more insidious. I wanted to scream. I couldn't sleep. I wanted the world to know everything I knew, but every good journalist knows: you've gotta read before you write and you can't break a big story without corroboration. So when I returned to the United States, I stole some fire from that contractor's tale and I followed his lead.

# 10. MARCH 2008– SEPTEMBER 2019

## AMERICA

9/11 was an inside job.

—GRAFFITI FROM THE WAR

I don't want to forget my father's advice. When I returned from Iraq, I sold three stories to my hometown newspaper, the *Winchester Star*. Tom Byrd, the *Star*'s editor, agreed to publish them as front pagers, starting with a big Saturday spread in early April 2008 headlined "Area man helps reverse Haditha fortune, image." Diet was that "area man," and I was the "Winchester-area native" who had traveled through red tape and sandstorms to find his friend in the middle of the Global War on Terror. But something was missing in these articles.

That being said, I felt like my father was proud of me as a writer for the first time in my life, and it meant the world. My father is my hero. He spent his life caring for strangers, and now these local strangers were telling him his son had done good work. His patients delivered laminated copies of the *Winchester Star* articles to his office. Beverly Sherwood, a Republican member of the Virginia House of Delegates, sent us a congratulatory note on official House stationery. Tom Byrd sent me a check for $500 and asked if I'd be willing to pose with Diet for a photo in a few weeks when we were both scheduled to return home for the Apple Blossom Festival.

I told Diet about all of this, and we laughed over the phone about the laminating and the letter from Sherwood. We'd both worked for her 1994 campaign as Young Republicans from Sherando High School. For us, that campaign was not about politics or the integrity of the Republican Party or the future of America. No, it was just an excuse to get out of the house and drink beer in the orchards with girls before halfheartedly performing our roles as serious young men at handshake functions with stodgy elders. But here we were again being asked to perform, and every year I think we do a better job of playing our parts. And it scares the hell out of me.

We agreed to the photo op. I drove home for the festival. For Apple Blossom weekend, the privileged all dress up in pink and green, just like the blooming trees. They put the most attractive and well-connected girls from the local high schools in pink satin dresses and assign them military escorts and station them on floats and invite third-tier celebrities from all over the country to lead prayer breakfasts and to be grand marshals and help us usher in the spring. There's something wonderfully pagan about the Apple Blossom Festival, this bacchanalia in the name of nature, but there's also an element of the absurd and the tragic in that Winchester, the former apple capital of the country, has pretty much cut down all its apple trees and replaced them with McMansions and suburban streets named after the fallen orchards. If this were a novel, Chuck Norris would have been Winchester's grand marshal in 2008 and he would have autographed my bicep and given Diet a high five. But that's not how the story went. Diet showed up at my parents' house at seven in the morning to pick me up for the Apple Blossom 10K, the race we would run prior to the parade and the photo op that would happen near Midway, the spot on our downtown mall where you could win big stuffed animals by popping balloons with darts and where you could munch on corn dogs and funnel cake while the ghosts of your childhood tacked about the streets drunk on spring and opioids and beer while semifamous people like Kirk Cameron drove by throwing candy to kids, like soldiers did in Iraq.

"Give me a hug," my mother said to Diet when he arrived at the door in the bright morning light.

Diet's Iraq mustache was gone. My grandfather had died the previous month, and thus I'd never had a chance to ask him about the mysterious bug in his hat, but my mother was still alive and all her hair was back, and my friend was alive, too. Diet stepped inside, he hugged my mother and shook my father's hand, and, among our barking dogs and other friends who were scheduled to run the race, I could feel nothing but the glow of home for a few precious moments.

"Welcome back," my father said to Diet.

We stood around the kitchen in that feeling of a father's pride and the smell of coffee, bacon, and French toast. We talked about Iraq and how everything was getting better. My mother had cried the previous night when I'd hugged her before bed, and I myself felt on the verge of tears when seeing all of us alive and together in the kitchen. The Apple Blossom Festival of 2008 now feels more than a little absurd when I remember the million Rockwellian tableaus of triumph and homecoming, that Make America Great Again vision of white, smiling America patting itself on the back in the morning light of kitchens and diners and parades. But the self-licking ice cream cone didn't feel absurd in the moment. The market had not yet crashed. I had not yet lost my job at A&T. James Foley had not yet been beheaded by ISIS on TV. Europe had not yet been rocked by the worst refugee crisis in a generation. And the burn pit victims weren't yet coming out of the woodwork. For a brief instant that morning, the war was over and I felt like I'd arrived at a happy ending. I'd sold my first story. My father was proud of me. My mother was alive. Diet was alive. I was alive. Mission accomplished.

But of course the mission was not accomplished, and I realized that as soon as Diet and I began to stretch for the race in the wet grass beside the city high school we'd once vandalized as teenagers. It was just before the race began when I finally asked him what he thought of the stories in the newspaper. He shook his head and swished his tongue beneath his teeth like he was searching for the annoying final shreds of an old wad of tobacco.

"Eat Boy, let's talk about it later," he said.

"What?" I said. "What did I miss?"

"It's not a big deal," he said. "Don't worry about it."

But I did worry about it. From his point of view, I'd gotten something wrong. And I wanted to get the story right. Diet and I got drunk that day. We never showed up for the *Winchester Star* photo op. After the brief reprieve of that Saturday morning moment of hugs in the bright Armstrong kitchen, we ran that race and returned to our contentious competitive positions about exactly what the story should be. We argued about the Haditha massacre. We argued about using the word *Haditha*. We argued about the WMDs. Diet still thought I'd been played by the contractor, and he told me to forget about it, but that wasn't the source of his problem with the stories in the *Winchester Star*, because I hadn't mentioned a word about the contractor or WMDs. I could never get a proper bead on exactly what Diet felt was missing from those articles, but after corresponding with Moni a few months later and sending the stories to her (and never hearing back), the mystery began to eat at me. I knew something was missing.

Although I sold those three stories to Tom Byrd, I kept the best three to myself. The ones I sold to the *Star* told of a heroic "area man," the Iraqi SWAT cops his men were training, and the girls' school America had blown up and was now helping to rebuild. The three I still wanted to tell involved the burn pits, the American education of Khalid Sheikh Mohammed in Greensboro, and the secret discovery of WMDs at the base of the Haditha dam in the summer of 2007. But here's the rub: How do you tell a story you don't fully know? And when, since we only live one life, do we ever fully know any story?

The silence of Diet and Moni told me the same thing my father's pride in my stories told me: I hadn't gone far enough. So I decided to go further. And I'd be lying if I said there was a method to the madness of "going further," but beyond simply doing a lot of background reading and talking with every veteran I could, there was a simple thing I kept doing over and over that seemed to help. I started telling the real stories. Over and over again. In every class I taught at North Carolina A&T I would begin by telling the beginning of this story: how I had to travel seven thousand miles away from home to find out the history of my own backyard. I wanted my students to know what I was just starting to realize: that the world was a strange and mysterious place and that the dead streets of Greensboro were not dead at all but alive with history and intrigue. Khalid Sheikh Mohammed, the mastermind of 9/11 and the highest-ranking Al Qaeda operative imprisoned at Guantánamo Bay, had received his entire American education in North Carolina, and the vast bulk of that study was conducted at A&T, the historically black college in Greensboro. The Global War on Terror was not just a remote debate between white policy wonks and dark crazy clerics, and it was not just about one side having WMDs and the other being the last great hope for civilization. No, in many ways the Global War on Terror was a story that started with a young man named Khalid who traveled seven thousand miles away from his home in Kuwait to see the other side of the world and saw more than he'd bargained for. The only question was, what was that "more"? If there was a dominant narrative of the Global War on Terror, what were the unofficial stories that were dying to be told?

"What the fuck happened to him?" a student asks every year.

And in that recurrent question is an echo of the best advice my father ever gave me, that simple question: "What about *them*?"

One night in 2010 I took a drive through Greensboro to a street called Montrose. Right before the Harris Teeter grocery store I turned right onto Montrose Drive off of West Market Street and followed the road back to what used to be called Colonial Apartments. I turned left into the complex and sought out the former address of Khalid Sheikh Mohammed: 333-B.

I remember swishing that address around in my head, telling myself not to fall prey to magical thinking. Three plus three plus three equals nine. B is the second letter of the alphabet. Nine plus two equals eleven. Welcome to the former home of the man who took down the twin towers on 9/11. Welcome to the front door of the uncle of Ramzi Yousef, the first person to try to take down the towers, in February 1993.

"Sir?" I said to an olive-skinned man in a white button-down shirt on a cell phone sitting on his front step under the stars.

"Yes?" he said, putting his hand over the phone.

"I'm a journalist," I said. "Can I ask you a few questions?"

His face went sour at the word *journalist*. He took his hand off the phone, stuck it out at me like a traffic cop. He turned around and went back inside.

This was not a promising start, but here was what I knew as of that night. Back in 1984, shortly after KSM arrived in Greensboro, he got into a traffic accident. I found a copy of the ticket ("FAILURE TO REDUCE SPEED") in the Guilford County clerk's office in 2009. KSM had apparently fender-bendered a woman named DeLois Christian Davis near 606 Benbow Road, a street within a few blocks of where I taught every day on what many folks still called the "dark side" of town.

I took pictures of 333-B, scribbled notes in my journal about the bland, cookie-cutter condos with their scraggly thickets, a standard greenery to me that might have been bewildering to KSM with his habituation to the desert environment of Kuwait. As I poked around that parking lot, I noticed a large number of the residents appeared to be Middle Eastern, and I knew I needed to find someone willing to talk, but that anonymous resident on his cell phone was not the only person who brushed me off. I'd also received the cold shoulder from Dr. Edward Fort, the university chancellor during KSM's time as a student. In December 2009, when I'd made FOIA requests to David Hardy of the FBI, I received no documents in return, which was strange because documents obviously existed. I'd made friends with a woman who worked in the registrar's office at A&T, and she had searched for KSM's files but claimed that those files, unlike all of his classmates' files, were gone, taken by the FBI.

I got back in my car, a gray Honda Civic, for whatever it's worth. As I turned east on Market toward home, I noticed a plaza to my left and a flashing neon sign for a hookah bar called Madina. I decided to give Madina a shot. I was feeling tense, like maybe a few puffs and a glass of tea might do me some good, and who knows? Where there's a hookah, there just might be a few men who might know something about this infamous man with the missing files.

Inside I smelled cologne, perhaps a touch of Axe, as well as a fruity smoke, and I noticed a number of Middle Eastern–looking guys puffing and talking, a few young fellows laughing and dancing, one even atop a table. I talked to a gorgeous black-haired woman named Christie who was operating the cash register, and I told her I was a journalist who was trying to find someone who might have known Khalid Sheikh Mohammed twenty years ago when he lived in Colonial Apartments.

"Who exactly is that?" she asked.

"The mastermind of 9/11," I said. "He used to live around the corner."

"Really?" she said.

"Really," I said.

"Let me talk to Andy," she said.

She walked behind a door and into either an office or a kitchen and returned with a thin, well-dressed man whose slick black hair and dark complexion did not scare me at all. I have never felt threatened in the Muslim community in Greensboro, but I did sometimes wonder if the warm feeling was reciprocal.

"What do you wish to know?" Andy asked.

I told Andy what I told Christie and I watched his face go solemn. He crossed his arms. His body language indicated caution, but he shook his head and said to me, "You should talk to that man in the back with his son. He may know something. He may not."

Seated at the final low table at the back of the hookah bar was a short, bald man whose diminutive stature reminded me a bit of Sheikh D'han Hussein D'meithan Al Jughayfi, the father I'd met in Haditha, the one who lived downstream from the burn pit. He stood up and shook my hand, said his name was Khaled. He introduced me to his son, who at that time was working at the Piedmont Triad International Airport.

"I did not know him," Khaled told me. "But I was here at that time, studying at North Carolina."

"A&T?" I asked.

"Yes," he said.

For about forty-five minutes Khaled and I chatted over deliciously sweet cups of chai tea, ghostly pelts of cherried smoke drifting around the room. I wondered if he thought I was CIA. I wondered if I was the first white man with a nickel pad to walk into Madina to interrogate customers about KSM. Like I said, for about forty-five minutes I was the one asking questions and Khaled was the one giving answers until something changed. Nearly an hour into the conversation, Khaled finally asked me a question: "Why do you want to know about him?"

I told Khaled what I've related here. I told him about Moni and my father and my time in Haditha and how I thought our country was blind and that I was not excepted from that condition, but I wanted to resist it to whatever extent I could. I wanted to know the real story about how this all started. I remember a long pause before Khaled said, "He was a friend of mine."

Just like that, on a weeknight in the middle of nowhere, a door flies open. Khaled's son straightened up and looked at his father, seemingly aware of the risk in that moment, that admission from his father.

"The first thing you need to know," Khaled said, "was that he was the little guy. You know what I mean? Very short. Always having to prove himself. But he was also very funny and smart. He had good sense of humor."

Khaled told me that Khalid was the youngest child in his family and that Khalid's father was an imam, a preacher, and that the family all saved up to send Khalid to America. He told me that his friend had transferred to North Carolina A&T from a North Carolina Baptist college in Murfreesboro called Chowan.

I followed that lead. Hungry to know what had happened in Murfreesboro, I visited Chowan and interviewed people in Murfreesboro, took pictures of yearbooks, and had Frank Timberlake, KSM's former roommate, hang up on me when I tried to find out the story behind his roommate's departure from Chowan. Later, from digging around in the work of other journalists, including Moni's, I discovered that most of the Muslim students at Chowan lived in a building called Parker Hall and often prayed in the Chowan chapel on Fridays and that a number of the white athletes liked to lean garbage cans full of water against the chapel doors and "n—— knock" on the Muslim students and then run away, swiping the Muslim students' shoes and throwing them into Lake Vann, a small body of water located next to the school's football field.

Yes, here was one way to interpret the inception of the Global War on Terror: this is a bully narrative. KSM had been bullied like an American nerd by the American jocks, and after fighting with our forces against the Soviets in Afghanistan, KSM returned to Kuwait to find those same forces occupying his home country in preparation for their first invasion of Iraq; local college bullying was now national military bullying. And so KSM began to develop a plot to bully back. He sent his nephew to bomb the World Trade Center two years after the 1991 Iraq war came to an end, and when those bombs didn't succeed in bringing down the towers, he used our own airplanes and Al Qaeda's network of radicals to finish the job on September 11. On that day KSM finally got his revenge. And now we're getting revenge for that revenge, at Guantánamo Bay and elsewhere. Is that too simple? I suspect it is. But there's something there: a part of the story.

"But what about them?" my father asked. "Who's their good guy? Who's their George Washington?"

How strange it seemed to me that my father's question guided me to Iraq and back, and not just back to Winchester and Greensboro but to Murfreesboro and hookah bars and bakeries and mosques and all over the library and back in time to the beginning of American history, the story of George Washington and the American Revolution. The deeper I dug into KSM's history, the more subversive my father's advice seemed. In early arraignment reports from Guantánamo Bay (disclosed by WikiLeaks), KSM tells the American military tribunal in Cuba that he sees himself as a Washingtonian figure. Not a terrorist but a revolutionary in the mold of our own founding father. "Because war, for sure," he says, "there will be victims." He says, "You know 40 million people were killed in World War I. Ten million killed in World War II. You know that two million four hundred thousand killed in the Korean War. So this is the language of war." But then KSM goes further with a rhetorical move that I find more than a little unsettling:

> When you said I'm a terrorist, I think it is deceiving peoples. Terrorists, enemy combatant. All these definitions as CIA you can make whatever you want. . . . I'm not happy that three thousand been killed in America. I feel sorry even. I don't like to kill children and the kids. Never Islam give me green light to kill peoples. Killing, as in the Christianity, Jews, and Islam, are prohibited. But there are exception of rule when you are killing people in Iraq. You said we have to do it. We don't like Saddam. But this is the way to deal with Saddam. Same thing you are saying. Same language you use, I use. When you are invading two-thirds of Mexico, you call your war manifest destiny. It up to you to call it what you want. But other side are calling you oppressors. If now George Washington, if now we were living in the Revolutionary War and George Washington he being arrested through Britain, for sure

he, they would consider him enemy combatant. But American they consider him as hero.

As I read this speech from this "detainee" who graduated from the historically black college where I, a white guy, taught, I felt a profound mix of emotions. I felt like a traitor for simply listening to the voice of the man who killed so many people on 9/11. But I also felt like I wanted to know more, and as a student of history and a son trying to be faithful to his father's advice, I *needed* to know more. Put in simple terms, I felt the two most fundamental geopolitical questions of our time were "How did we get in this mess?" and "How do we get out?" In other words, what was it that ushered in the Global War on Terror and how can America extract itself from the rhetoric and the budgets that have attended this disastrous campaign without considering the lives—the stories—of the people on the other side?

"You are funny. You should write about something funny," my father would say whenever I called and shared my most recent KSM story or a finding abut the burn pits or another chemical weapons discovery.

"Eat Boy," Diet would say, "humor is your strength. You should write about something else. Write fiction. Write a funny song like that guy Arlo Guthrie, that one about the pickle and the motorcycle."

But as much as I enjoy the warm and zany songs of Arlo Guthrie, I relate more deeply to his rebellious father, Woody, the guy who sang "This Land Is Your Land." Of course the hidden message in Diet's advice could simply be that I, Eat Boy, am broken, my light spirit losing its light, or maybe I have become the controlling figure I'm describing him as and that his desire for me to write about something other than this war is not a function of him feeling threatened by me so much as Diet being exhausted from having spent the entirety of his adult life not telling but *living* "the story of the war." The Forever War.

It breaks my heart that this might be the case, and it makes me want to return to the safety of comedy and the zany voices and pranks of child-hood, the security of that old Eat Boy role. Diet and I struggle to maintain our friendship. I, too, with little more than a fortnight of experience in a war zone, feel exhausted by the echoes and implications of what my country has done, and I do find myself craving play and laughter, but I also feel that good friends, just like good partners and good citizens, do not just say "yes, dear" or "thank you for your service" to the ones they love. Good friends take an active interest in each other. They challenge each other with a spirit of love and purpose. So when Diet asks for funny songs, I do sometimes say, "I'll get right on that," and I'll mean it, but other times I'll remind Diet of this unsettling truth: KSM's own friends and the witnesses to his arraignment at Guantánamo Bay have said the mastermind of 9/11's most salient personality trait is his sense of humor. The recurrent thread in the story of observers and friends was that KSM was a joker, that he had a wicked sense of humor. His role in his social group was, in a way, like my role in mine. His friends claimed that he was a great impersonator of Americans and that he often led his comrades in a series of charades on Friday nights in Greensboro in the mid-1980s, a weekly skit show they called "Friday Night Live." Based on NBC's long-running TV show *Saturday Night Live*, KSM's group of Greensboro friends would meet on Fridays, because Friday was Islam's holy day. I know something I suspect KSM also knows: sometimes a sense of humor is not the way out of the dark but the way into forgetting that the people you're talking about are people.

On my best days I know this: I do not want to be part of the amnesia, the book of laughter and forgetting. After the market crashed and funding for our interdisciplinary writing program dried up, I got laid off by North Carolina A&T and began teaching at a community college. It was there that a student told me she lived in KSM's old complex, that her landlord had been questioned by the FBI after KSM's arrest, and that the only thing the landlord could remember about KSM and his friends was that their neighbors were always calling in complaints on them because they often brought a live goat home from a neighboring farm and killed it in the apartment on Fridays before their skits and their feasts. The sound of the bleats and the sight of the blood was sometimes a bit much for their American neighbors.

"Dad," I would say, "they called him Belushi, like John Belushi from SNL, because he was their leader, yeah, but also because he was originally from Baluchistan, Pakistan."

More often than not it was my mother, not my father, who wanted to hear me nerd out about these stories of the war. The closer my mother got to death, the more she wanted to have fearlessly honest conversations about everything. My father, on the other hand, seemed torn between pride over the extent to which I had followed his advice and fear over the way these discoveries chipped away at the easy humor and simple patriotism he had raised me on during the Cold War. But my father has also evolved beyond that simple past, if he ever truly lived there at all. Ultimately it was the wisdom of his question that had sent me on a journey that was far more profound than any plane ticket.

I intend to see the journey of that question through. What I mean by that is that I am trying to keep my heart and mind open to the people whom a good number of people in my country want to erase, kill, or confine in camps. When I returned from Iraq, I saw Iraq, Syria, Kuwait, Pakistan, Iran, Afghanistan—the modern Middle East—everywhere I looked. We were killing these people every day, and now we're drifting down into Africa, and I just can't be that American who shuts his eyes and thereby extends a blank check to a government to torture and continually use drones to play whack-a-mole with a group of human beings who just happen to not be white. So, in spite of feeling the fear of Diet and my father—that I might be in danger of losing my sacred sense of humor—I continued to dig. I began work on a book about KSM's time in Greensboro, a week in his life organized around the explosion of the *Challenger* space shuttle in 1986. Here, prior to 9/11, was KSM's introduction to Americans' fascination with death on television. We had the Kennedy assassination, the *Challenger* explosion, and 9/11. These were the three big ones, the symbolic American catastrophes we can't stop putting on instant replay. One of the astronauts who was on the *Challenger* was Ronald McNair, another graduate of North Carolina A&T, and so when the *Challenger* blew up and all the astronauts were killed on national television and all of white America wanted to eulogize Christa McAuliffe (the woman who would have been the first citizen astronaut), Jesse Jackson visited his alma mater to eulogize McNair. Because Jackson was considered a contender for the 1988 Democratic presidential nomination, I imagined a young KSM watching this black man eulogizing this forgotten black hero while a predominantly white media swarmed around both Jackson and KSM, teaching the young engineer and future media operations chief of Al Qaeda a number of valuable lessons about what America truly values. I imagined KSM after the eulogy playing whack-a-mole at a local arcade and wondering why there were no Muslims on the shuttle and no blacks on TV and why America likes to watch people die on TV, over and over.

"I don't want to get killed," my agent said to me when I submitted an early draft of my KSM manuscript to him.

I published a chapter called "Phantom Jets" and titled the book *The Challenger*. I became obsessed with hearing the story of the man nobody in Greensboro wanted to acknowledge. Here, I thought, was the elephant in the room. I wanted to know what it was like to be KSM at an HBCU in the American South during the Reagan years. I wanted to know what it was like for the most notorious murderer of my generation to be a student at the college that started the sixties with a spirit of peaceful protest. How and why did that spirit turn violent? How bad was the bullying and racism in the eighties in North Carolina? And why did I care about a man nobody else seemed to care about? I suppose I should just come out and acknowledge another elephant in the room of this story.

I know that my obsession with this war on terror and with KSM was at least in part a coping mechanism for avoiding the specter of my mother's death. I was not always oblivious to the way I played a strange game of whack-a-mole with my own pain over my mother's cancer, but it wasn't just her dying that propelled me forward into the darkest stories of the Forever War. After my mother's cancer returned a fourth, fifth, and sixth time, I underwent a genetic screening to see if I had the same mutation as her, the BRCA2 gene, and guess what I found out? I'm a mutant. I've got a much greater chance of getting cancer than most other people, and as the stories about the burn pits started to leak and break, I started to think about Captain Al'a and his fearless mullet, and I started to feel the fundamental truth and guarantee of life: it ends. We all die. The seed of sickness blooms within me like a strange and patient fruit. I am going to die. Just like you. To paraphrase Jim Morrison, none of us gets out of here alive. I used to call my band Viva la Muerte—long live death—because it sounded cool, but now I feel that name age in strange ways and feel that the sooner we come to grips with that guarantee, the sooner we can start living each day like it's our last and thereby do something purposeful and bold before it's too late.

For me this meant pursuing the truth and finding the real story about Haditha, my grandfather, KSM, the burn pits, and the WMDs, and it also meant driving home to see my mother and father whenever I could and being absolutely sincere and honest with both of them about just how much I loved them. When Uncle Carl and Aunt Susan wrote me a letter to tell me that I might want to write to my mother before it was too late, I took that advice and I wrote a ten-page howl that day, and when I picked up the phone to hear my mother crying, I cried too, and it felt good, and once the tears came out, the sense of humor was allowed back. My mother told me she'd had a dream that week in which she'd seen magnificent colors and spinning wheels, and she wondered if these were like the rainbow things I'd seen when I was misbehaving with psychedelic drugs as a young man. I laughed. She laughed. I told her to tell me more. She said the dream had filled her with a radiance, an energy, a desire to wake up and make my father a gigantic breakfast of pancakes and bacon with an egg right smack dab in the middle of it all, a sort of breakfast mandala.

"So it felt good?" I said.

"It felt wonderful," she said. "But then I just couldn't even make it to the kitchen."

This makes me both happy and sad to remember. My mother's spirit—her desire to serve others—was strong right up until the end. Right up until her final weeks she was dreaming of making a feast for others, wondering if her dream might connect her to the dreams of her children. Not to sound platitudinal, but she was the most wonderful mother a son could ever have, the fire of our family. And so when my father told me that I might want to come home for the second weekend of November because it might be goodbye, I took my father's advice and drove north up Route 220 to Route 81 and scrawled notes about KSM and the burn pits and WMDs in my journal as I drove with Yorick, my corgi, in the shotgun seat, sitting atop this constantly jarred journal with its slanty chicken scratch about cancerous veterans and terrorist detainees and angry contractors who nobody in the world wanted to hear about except for you, whoever you are who is reading this.

I drove through the Shenandoah Valley, where the Shawano Indians—the Shawnee—used to live. America has a done a great job of banishing its dark history—its dark people—to the pale rim of our national narratives, but my mother was one of those women who wanted those stories told. When I was a child, she would point out the dark green splotches on the country club golf courses where you could still detect the outlines of the Shawnee burial mounds, the marks of those vanquished bodies. Like my father with his question of "What about them?" my mother's patriotism (she demanded that "America, the Beautiful" be sung at her funeral) was not made of simple fearful racist stuff. We hung a flag over our front door, and I was always proud to walk under it when I came home, and that night when I did, I hugged my father and walked back over the black slate tiles of the dimly lit hallway to the humidifier sound and pale wood of my parents' bedroom to kiss my mother goodnight.

The next day I took a break from raking leaves with my father to tell my mother one more time how much I loved her, and for some reason I got a notion to pick up an old comb I saw on the edge of her sink. As I combed my mother's hair the way she used to comb mine, I could hear my father coming around the side yard with his rake and moving into the backyard, just behind us, and I saw him out there behind the blinds against the old stones of the Civil War wall in our backyard and I timed my combs to his rakes. My mother couldn't speak anymore, but she could hear the sudden music of the rake in the grass and the comb in her hair, and I could tell she could tell by her smile.

My sister, Katee, who worked at a VA hospital in Richmond, walked into the house that evening and called out for our mother. She called for me. I told her I was upstairs, where I read to her a letter a fundamentalist cousin had written to my mother to alert her to the possibility that she—my mother—was about to go to hell if she didn't accept Jesus Christ as her savior immediately. My father and I kept that letter from my mother, and it was the sick reality of that cousin's love that my sister and I were discussing when my father came upstairs to tell us the news: our mother was dead.

I jumped into my father's arms and yelped out in such aquatic fashion that my sister laughed in the middle of her tears and compared the sound I'd made to that of a whale. For a moment, embryonically coiled in my father's lap, I sobbed. Then we all walked downstairs to say goodbye. My sister took a jade ring from my mother's finger and wears it to this day. My father called my brother down in Chapel Hill and made us lamb for dinner as the hospice worker arrived to remove my mother's body and her painkillers. Several days later Diet and all of my close friends from high school and college returned for my mother's funeral.

In my eulogy for my mother I told the story of how, when I was eleven years old and our house was burning down, my mother jumped into the flames and onto the burning tractor that was the cause of the fire and tried to drive that machine out of the garage before it exploded. All of my old friends, including Diet, called my mother "Wild Mary K" because she did stuff like that. She had a wild spirit. My mother was a strong woman, and like a lot of the women in this story, my mother's strength had something to do with a hunger to connect with and tell the story of others. My earliest memory of her was of driving around Winchester, listening to her talk about "Papa," her father who had died when I was only a year old. My mother tried to keep his spirit alive by telling me stories about his kindness and wildness, as well as the fact that he smoked cigarettes. In those drives of earliest memory I remember her telling me how smoke can kill you, as it did Papa, and then taking me for walks on the downtown mall, where she would introduce me to folks from the old George Washington House, a mental hospital whose patients used to amble about in public in the early eighties as part of their therapy. My mother loved to introduce me to these people, and she took great delight in the shock on their faces when I'd tell them that they shouldn't smoke their cigarettes because smoking will give you a heart attack. What I emphasized in the eulogy was that my mother, from the very beginning, refused conventional wisdom and tried to teach me *how* to talk with strangers, not to be scared of them or avoid them. In my father's eulogy for my mother, he spoke of the same thing. He told that packed church that he was proud to have been married—and to have loved—a strong woman for forty-five years.

My mother and my father together, in their own way, taught me that strangers matter. Fearful as they may have been about losing their son in Iraq, the question their lives continually raise is, "What about them?" Indeed, what about others? Moni Basu, the "Evil Media Chick" I met at the beginning of my trip, risked her life over and over to tell the stories of the third-party nationals, the invisible foreign workers of the Iraq War. Lucy, the woman I met at the end of my trip who believed the world was plagued by tribalism, risked her life to return to Iraq and work with her people and plant gardens. Karen, whom many, I suspect, will like to think of as just a "stripper," is so much more than that. Growing up in a military town where men started and prosecuted and simulated war constantly, Karen fought her way out, emerging from an Old Testament Christian cult and teenage homelessness to become one of the most empathetic people I have ever met, a woman who is still my friend and would likely challenge me on describing her as a "woman" because Karen, just like Chelsea Manning and many others, now resists the binary categories of man and woman. Karen now dates a transgender individual whose name—Saryn—echoes the name of the chemical weapons the United States sold to Iraq to kill Iranians in the eighties. Karen is no longer a "she" but now identifies as "they." They, like my mother, cared deeply for others, and not just human beings like yours truly, but those invisible animals like the mice for which they built a home in their mother's house, that strange teeming colony enough to cause a rift between parent and child that contributed to Karen being kicked out of their mother's home at fifteen.

Something is wrong with the world we have created, and my mother knew it, and so did Moni, Lucy, and Karen. Like those in the mythical village from Ursula K. Le Guin's story "The Ones Who Walk Away from Omelas," we live in a world whose happiness and wealth *seem* to depend on keeping a single child alone and deprived—invisible and suffering—in a basement. What Le Guin describes in the basement of that story is what my mother sought to combat by constantly introducing her child to strangers. The estrangement needs to end. The blinders need to come off. The lesson for children should not be to not talk with strangers. We should not turn our backs on dark people or poor people or foreigners or the millions of species we eradicate with each passing year. Lobsters, polar bears, strippers, contractors, African Americans, Native Americans, Iraqis, Palestinians, Syrians, Kurds, Yemenis, Somalis, Mexicans, women worldwide, and the not-so-white men we continue to imprison without trial down at Guantánamo Bay all have this in common: they are often invisible to the old white privileged world that would have us believe that their suffering, extinction, and invisibility constitute a necessary precondition for American wealth, happiness, and security.

This is bullshit. This is a myth. Evil of course does exist. In each of us. But so does good. My mother and father instructed me to talk to strangers because they knew this myth of the chosen good and the chosen evil to be precisely that—a myth. And I tell you all of this because this fundamental wisdom of caring for strangers matters to me, just as it mattered to them, and because of what came next in the story of my friendship with Diet. When Diet told me after my mother's funeral that he wanted me to write his eulogy some day, he also asked me if I wanted to join him and his girlfriend in Vermont in December and take a skiing trip after New Year's. It felt good to feel appreciated for what I had written. I accepted the invitation and remember nothing but laughter for most of the trip, which began in Boston, where Diet was getting a master's degree from the JFK School of Government at Harvard.

"What was up with the ending to that story you just sold?" he asked me that first night after I arrived in Boston.

I was glad he'd taken the time to read my work. I had indeed recently sold a piece to *Esquire*, and it involved a soldier and her unemployed boyfriend and contained an explicit and deviant ending that complicated the reader's relationship to the trauma the female protagonist experienced while serving in Iraq.

"You liked it?" I asked.

"It was definitely weird," he said. "Definitely Eat Boy."

In that moment I wanted to do what storytellers are never supposed to do. I wanted to explain myself. But I didn't. I wanted to keep the good feeling going. It was December 2013. More than six hundred thousand Iraqis had been killed in the war, but again I felt like Iraq was in the past, history finally sealed up in a nice tight little package. I noticed carpets from all over the world in Diet's two-story house in Cambridge, intricate tribal rugs from Pakistan and Afghanistan.

"We're going to a party tomorrow night," Diet said. "If that's okay with you."

I took off my shoes and sat by the warm light of the fire and let Diet pour me a tall glass of bourbon. I wondered if what he meant was, "Do you feel like being social in light of your mom's death?"

I told him I wanted to go. I may explore the past in my writing, but I don't like to wallow in it in my life any more than I have to. I want to move on, as they say. And I wanted the same for my country. But as William Faulkner once wrote, "The past is never dead. It's not even past." It keeps rearing its head like that whack-a-mole in the old eighties arcade game.

The next day Diet and I walked all over the cobblestones of Boston in the cold Charles River air, moving in vectors from heated bar to heated bar. We talked about mothers and girlfriends and the counterculture icon, the scientist-prankster Stewart Brand. We stepped inside a thrift store, where I found a vintage leather jacket with a belt and big buttons and garish furry lapels, the kind of garment you might find on a pimp or a disco singer in the late seventies. I decided to wear it to the party, where it probably suggested to the host that I was pretty far from a serious person. Maybe I wanted to prove to Diet I hadn't lost my sense of humor, that I was still a prankster. Maybe I'm always trying to prove something to someone because that's the kind of man I am.

In any event, we went to the party. The host was a wealthy white guy who lived in a well-appointed home not far from Diet's. His name was Frank Thorp IV, and he was retired navy, a former national security advisor in the Bush administration. I watched him drink and laugh with the rest of the white guests, and I was constantly turning over a phrase Diet had shared with me from the heated discussions he'd encountered in the Harvard classrooms: "Check your privilege."

This phrase summarized a race-, class-, and gender-conscious movement that was sweeping across the country. Well, here was privilege going largely unchecked: whiteness bantering with whiteness in a Boston brownstone. Scotch and champagne, scallops on silver platters. I watched Diet talk with his young and attractive white classmates from the JFK School of Government. I wondered, as I often do, if Diet would one day take a stab at politics. I hope he does. Because in spite of the privileged blinders we both wear, I think our country could use a leader who has actually lived among the poor and war-torn people we've occupied for these past nineteen years, a man who understands cost in terms other than dollars.

Diet checked on me throughout the night, asking if I was okay. Around midnight Frank Thorp IV came out from behind his bar and offered me a drink and introduced himself. Diet mentioned that I was in a rock band. I mentioned that I also occasionally did some journalism and that I'd embedded with Diet's JSOF unit in Haditha. Just before 2013 turned into 2014, Thorp toasted me and graciously thanked both Diet and me for our service. Then, in the first minutes of 2014, we talked about Iraq. Thorp didn't say anything about the burn pits or ISIS or the rash of beheadings or the television images of refugees swarming the Syrian, Turkish, or German borders. Those horrific visions were still a few months away, at least for me. In the last seconds of 2013 Iraq felt like a bullet I'd dodged, like a mess Diet and Thorp had helped to clean up, like a problem that had largely been solved. I liked Frank Thorp, the decent, appreciative feeling he gave off, that of soldiers and journalists both being essential to democracy. As the conversation progressed, he told me that his wife, Tamara, had broken the story of the Iraq invasion through NBC. He winked at me when I asked him how she got the lead. When I told him about the KBR contractor's story, Thorp nodded and smiled. Although his understanding of events suggested that the weapons cache belonged to the sons of Saddam and not Chemical Ali, he did confirm the discovery of a massive, classified weapons trove at the base of the Haditha dam in the summer of 2007.

I didn't betray my excitement about finally getting corroboration from a former national security advisor to George Bush. But the last thing I did before I went to bed that night in Boston was drop to my knees in my guest bedroom and jot down my notes from the conversation. In the coming weeks I would submit my story to newspapers all over the country, including the *New York Times*. Roughly nine months later, during the same week that C. J. Chivers of the *New York Times* broke his Pulitzer Prize–winning story about Iraq's chemical weapons program and its mysterious connections to American sources, I published my story in *The Mantle*.

I was furious that Chivers had scooped me, especially after having submitted my story to his newspaper. I sometimes felt paranoid, believing that the true WMD narrative was being glossed over with simplistic official mythology, as was the case with so many stories past (the JFK assassination, the Manson murders, the Central Park Five). However, as I read over Chivers's work, my feelings changed. Chivers was a far superior journalist, with excellent sources from his service as a marine. Although I felt that his service at times compelled an overly cautious voice about these weapons discoveries, his caution and decency have aged well, and I was ultimately glad to see the country having a public conversation, albeit a very brief one, about Iraq and its WMDs, as ISIS's murderous campaign was making it abundantly clear that this war was still not over. Furthermore, I found it interesting that Chivers left out the Haditha discovery and that in his Global War on Terror chronicle, *The Fighters* (2018), Haditha is not mentioned once.

And so that city on the Euphrates still remains a mystery and so does the story of the dam and the burn pits and KSM. The mastermind of 9/11 has still not received a trial, and it makes me wonder, What are we afraid of, America? In 2015 Donald Trump launched his campaign for the presidency with a promise to not just keep Guantánamo Bay open but to double down and fill it back up. Guantánamo Bay is thus still a monument to America's fears and its disregard for the rule of law. That same year I was asked to co-teach a course at Duke University called Revolution and Terror. Using simulations (games), the class enacted the stories of figures like George Washington, Karl Marx, Ted Kaczynski, Osama bin Laden, and KSM. I had recently written a book review of *Murder at Camp Delta*, Joseph Hickman's whistle-blower account of the atrocities he had witnessed as a watchtower guard at Guantánamo, KSM's new home, and Hickman and I had developed enough of a friendship that he agreed to Skype into the Duke classroom to talk to the students.

They asked Joe about the Global War on Terror, torture, secret prisons, ISIS, and if he had trouble sleeping at night. They gave him a rousing ovation for blowing the whistle on America's most notorious prison, and I took a picture of Joe smiling on a big screen over the faces of my students who couldn't believe they'd been given the chance to have a conversation with a whistle-blower. These young people were not the stereotypical apathetic American amnesiacs you sometimes read about in the media's discourse on millennials. These students cared. They read. They were angry. They wanted to know the truth. A few hours after the conversation, Hickman told me on the phone that he'd enjoyed talking to the students much more so than any of the journalists who had interviewed him for magazines like *Newsweek*. I thanked him not just for speaking with my class and sharing his firsthand accounts but also for standing up for Ali Abdullah Ahmed, Mani al-Utabyi, and Yasser al-Zahrani, three men whom Hickman claimed government contractors had murdered at Guantánamo Bay. I admired Hickman for putting his life and career on the line for these strangers. When I asked him what his next book was going to be about, he asked me, "Have you heard of the burn pits?"

I told him what I had seen in Haditha.

"You were in a bad place, my friend," he said.

Hickman told me that he and a number of the guards and detainees at Guantánamo Bay had read my work on KSM. When his second book, *The Burn Pits*, came out, I read through it as quickly as I did the first, and I couldn't believe how America was playing out the same story over and over again like some child who refused to grow up—how we were denying the truth of the burn pits in the same way we had with Agent Orange and Gulf War syndrome.

Like a lot of service members I've met since my time in Haditha, Joe knows that our country is in trouble and that a great deal of this trouble goes back to our regime change wars in places like Iraq and the fact that Guantánamo Bay is still open and that we still don't have the courage to bring the mastermind of 9/11 to trial. Soldiers like Hickman share the anger of the contractor I met in Kuwait, as well as the skepticism and patriotism of Diet and my father. Whether it's the story of Edward Snowden or the howl of the now imprisoned Reality Winner or the rage of the anonymous military intelligence officer I recently met who told me I was just now touching the tip of the iceberg of Haditha, the story is largely the same: many of America's soldiers and intelligence officers increasingly feel betrayed by their leadership and feel our democracy is in danger. And Donald Trump has not made things better with his promises to build walls and double down on torture and secret prisons and drone attacks on African nations. As Chivers writes in *The Fighters*, "On one matter there can be no argument. The foreign policies that sent these men and women abroad, with an emphasis on military activities and visions of reordering foreign nations and cultures, did not succeed. It is beyond honest dispute that the wars in Afghanistan and Iraq failed to achieve what their organizers promised." Chivers is right. But from where I'm sitting today in Greensboro, North Carolina, that failure—the entire story of the Global War on Terror—can still seem academic if, by academic, we mean a conversation by elites constructed for elites, a series of intellectual walls created by priestly paternal figures to keep immature children from seeing that the bogeyman is, in fact, a human being.

No, for me this is about more than foreign policy. This is about more than making an academic point about geopolitics and torture, some elaborate thesis about the secret history of the Global War on Terror. For me, this is about knowing that the air of Iraq—the Haditha burn pit smoke—still lives inside of me. This is about knowing that fear personally and knowing that my brother, perhaps fueled by a fear of what that Iraqi-American air has done to his brother, is now working on detecting the epigenetic signature for burn pit cancers. This is about what it's like to be alive in America right now with its growing hunger for myths and walls, its denial and censorship of science, and its fear of evildoers from Africa, Mexico, and the Middle East sneaking into the country via swarthy "caravans." This is about a new normal where we all swallow twelve lies a day from Donald Trump. This is about a war that is still going on. This is about how every time I walk down Elm Street in Greensboro I see the black side of the city on one side (the east) and the white side (the west) on the other. This is about how every time I drive to the grocery store on West Market, I see a bakery on my left where Palestinian immigrants make the best lamb in town and where one of the proprietor's daughters (who wants to be a dentist) has taken to wearing a hijab since the election of Donald Trump. As I drive farther I see the old hookah bar where I met KSM's friend (it's now a grocery store), and I see the sign for Montrose Drive off to the right and I know that road leads back to a series of apartments where immigrants from Palestine, Syria, Afghanistan, and

Iraq live right now. Where Khalid Sheikh Mohammed once impersonated Americans in the 1980s, a new generation of refugees and immigrants now live, watching Donald Trump and America on their televisions and computer screens, waiting to see how these stories will unfold.

"Give? Give?" said those two young shepherd boys from Haditha I met in the middle of the desert on the day I thought I was going to die, those clouds of sheep swarming all around me.

"Give? Give?" the brothers said.

Their English was as limited as my Arabic. Those brothers held out their hands, looking left and right at Diet and me and all the other Americans with their sunglasses and guns. What became of those brothers and the air they breathe and the water they drink? My generation went to war in Iraq, and when the war went south, we tried to forget about Iraq. But I can't. I can't stop wondering: Is the Captain okay? Is the river okay? Are those brothers still alive? And if so, have they forgotten about us? I often think about them and the terror and wonder I felt when I saw them marching their sheep out of that desert sky. What kind of men have they become, and what became of that blue handkerchief and that one-dollar bill—that George Washington—I handed over to them when I had nothing else to give?